AQUINAS AND ANALOGY

Ralph McInerny

AQUINAS AND ANALOGY

The Catholic University of America Press
Washington, D.C.

The paper used in this publication meets the minimum requirements of
American National Standards for Information Science—Permanence of
Paper for Printed Library materials, ANSI Z39.48-1984.

∞

LIBRARY OF CONGRESS CATALOGING-IN-PUBLICATION DATA
McInerny, Ralph M.
    Aquinas and analogy / Ralph M. McInerny.
        p.   cm.
    Includes bibliographical references and index.
    1. Thomas, Aquinas, Saint, 1225?-1274.—Contributions in
doctrine of analogy. 2. Analogy—History. 3. Analogy (Religion)
—History of doctrines—Middle Ages, 600-1500. 4. Analogy
(Religion)—History of doctrines—16th century. 5. Cajetan,
Tommaso de Vio, 1469-1534—Contributions in doctrine of
analogy. I. Title.
B765.T54M236   1996
169'.092—dc20
96-16793
ISBN 0-8132-0848-3 (cloth: alk. paper)
ISBN 0-8132-0932-3 (pbk: alk. paper)

For David Burrell, C.S.C.
amicus amico

CONTENTS

PREFACE

Since publishing *The Logic of Analogy* in 1961, I have continued to think about and write on the subject, almost exclusively as it pertains to the teaching of Thomas Aquinas. Some of these writings were brought together in *Studies in Analogy* (1968). Both books have been out of print for a number of years and the question arose as to whether they should be reprinted. I decided that it would be preferable to treat the matter afresh. The result is this book. Like many others, I found Cardinal Cajetan's treatise on the subject oddly dissatisfying. It is no pleasure for a Thomist to depart from the views of so eminent a leader of the school, but *etiam Homerus dormitat* and when Cajetan nodded, his head hit the table. I have given here as clear a statement as I can of the nature of the great cardinal's mistake. The reader will find below my argument that Cajetan embraced the very fallacy Thomas was defusing in the text that provided the fundamental structure of the cardinal's treatise. After examining the role that analogy plays in the thought of Aristotle, and the degree to which Aristotelian analogy can be taken to be regulative of Thomas's usage, I move systematically through the topics that enable one to see the precise character of Thomas's teaching. I have tried to make this book as straightforward as I can. If I am wrong, the critic will have no trouble discerning his target. If I am correct, a good deal that has been, and continues to be, said about analogy in Thomas Aquinas is simply wrongheaded. The University of Notre Dame, where I have taught now for more than forty years, has been an ideal setting for my philosophical work. My colleagues in the Department of Philosophy have been both stimuli and edifiers over the years. I trust that the others will not take it amiss if I express my particular gratitude to David Burrell.

PART ONE

PROLEGOMENA

ONE

WHERE CAJETAN WENT WRONG

When Thomas de Vio completed his short work *De nominum analogia* on September 1, 1498, in the Dominican convent of St. Apollinaris in Padua, he had put the interpretation of what St. Thomas has to say about analogous names onto a path it still travels today. At twenty-nine years of age Cajetan was already an intellectual power. He was and is one of the great glories of the Thomistic school and it was, *pace* Gilson, entirely fitting that his commentary on the *Summa theologiae* should be printed along with that work in the Leonine Edition. Cajetan was to become master general of the Dominican Order as well as a cardinal, and he was chosen for the extremely delicate task of going north to reason with Martin Luther. If he failed to reconcile the fiery Augustinian friar with the Church, Cajetan was himself influenced by the newer approaches to Scripture. Indeed, he devoted the last years of his life to the composition of literal commentaries on the Bible, invoking the aid of the Jewish scholars of Rome.

But I have come to criticize Cajetan, not to praise him. My criticism is devoted exclusively to his presentation of St. Thomas's doctrine of the analogy of names. My criticism concentrates on, but is not confined to, the *De nominum analogia*,[1] whose structure depends on what Cajetan calls types or kinds of analogous name. It is essential to see that Cajetan is fundamentally mistaken in speaking of kinds of analogous name as he does. The distinction of analogous names into types, which we find in his little work, reposes on a fallacy. That is, Cajetan's influential threefold (or fourfold) division of analogous names is based on a mistake that vitiates what he has to say on analogous names in the opusculum and later.

De Nominum Analogia

After a brief preliminary remark in which he tells us of the need and importance of a correct understanding of analogous names, Cajetan notes that *analogia* is borrowed from the Greeks and can be rendered in Latin as *proportio* or *proportionalitas*. The term has come to be used in ways remote from its origin, however, a development that causes great confusion; to remedy this problem, Cajetan suggests that we approach the matter by first setting down a threefold division that proceeds from what is less properly to what is really and truly analogy. The division is: analogy of inequality, analogy of attribution, and analogy of proportionality.

Ad tres ergo modos analogiae omnia analoga reducuntur: scilicet ad analogiam inaequalitatis, et analogiam attributionis, et analogiam proportionalitatis. Quamvis secundum veram vocabuli proprietatem et usum

---

1. Thomas De Vio Cardinalis Caietanus, *Scripta Philosophica. De Nominum Analogia. De Conceptu Entis*, ed. P. N. Zammit, O.P., and P. H. Hering, O.P. (Rome: Angelicum, 1952). The literature on analogy in St. Thomas is vast. Other than my own previous work, *The Logic of Analogy* (The Hague: Martinus Nijhoff, 1961), and *Studies in Analogy* (The Hague: Martinus Nijhoff, 1968), I shall mention only Bernard Montagnes, O.P., *La doctrine de l'analogie de l'être d'après saint Thomas d'Aquin* (Paris–Louvain: Nauwelaerts, 1963); Giuseppe Casetta, ed., *Origini e Sviluppi dell'Analogia da Parmenide a S. Tommaso* (Firenze: Edizioni Vallombrosa, 1987); *Metafore dell'invisibile: Ricerche sull'analogia, Contributi al XXXIII Convegno del Centro di Studi filosofici di Gallarate* (Brescia: Morcelliana, 1983); Franco Riva, *L'analogia metaphorica: Una questione logico-metafisica nel tomismo* (Milano: Pubblicazioni dell'Università Cattolica, 1989); and Bruno Pinchard, *Métaphysique et Sémantique: Autour de Cajetan, Etude et Traduction du 'De Nominum Analogia'* (Paris: Vrin, 1987). In the present essay, I shall not be taking into account the secondary literature, a decision that is quantitative rather than qualitative.

Aristotelis, ultimus modus tantum analogiam constituat, primus autem alienus ab analogia omnino sit. (n. 3)

All analogous [terms] are reduced to three kinds of analogy: that is, to analogy of inequality, analogy of attribution, and analogy of proportionality. Nonetheless according to the true and correct sense of the term and Aristotle's use only the last kind constitutes analogy and the first is completely foreign to analogy.

This division is based on a text taken from St. Thomas's commentary on the *Sentences* of Peter Lombard where the question at issue is: Are all things true by uncreated truth? When creatures are said to be true, are they being referred to the Truth God is, being named from Him, or can they be called true on the basis of something in themselves, so that there is not one single truth that explains calling things true but a plurality of truths answering to the plurality of true things? The text on which Cajetan built his interpretation is an answer to the following objection, the first that St. Thomas poses.

Videtur quod omnia sint vera una veritate quae est veritas increata. Sicut enim dictum est in solutione praecedentis articuli, verum dicitur analogice de illis in quibus est veritas, sicut sanitas de omnibus sanis. Sed una est sanitas numero a qua denominatur animal sanum, sicut subjectum ejus, et medicina sana, sicut causa ejus, et urina sana, sicut signum ejus. Ergo videtur quod una sit veritas qua omnia dicuntur vera. (*I Sent.* d. 19, q. 5, a. 1, obj.1)

It seems that all true things are true by that one truth that is uncreated truth. For, as was said in the solution of the preceding article, true is said analogically of those things in which truth is, as health is of all healthy things. But there is numerically one health whereby the animal is denominated healthy as its subject, and medicine healthy as its cause, and urine healthy as its sign. So it seems there is one truth whereby all are called true.

The argument is clear enough. Pluto, his vitamins, and his urine are called healthy analogously, and we can see that they are so denominated from the health that is a quality only in Pluto; there is no need to look for a plurality of healths, one the quality of the dog, another the quality of the medicine, the other the quality of urine. These several things are gathered under one name because medicine *causes* and urine *shows* the quality health in the animal. If this is the case with the analogous term 'healthy' and if 'true' is said to be analogically common to God and creature, it seems to follow that there must be numerically one truth in virtue of which this is done.

The assumption is that a feature of the things called healthy is a necessary condition of their being named analogously, so that wherever there is an analogous name that feature will be present. Thomas replies:

Ad primum igitur dicendum, quod aliquid dicitur secundum analogiam tripliciter: [1] *vel secundum intentionem tantum, et non secundum esse*; et hoc est quando una intentio refertur ad plura per prius et posterius, quae tamen non habet esse nisi in uno; sicut intentio sanitatis refertur ad animal, urinam et diaetam diversimode, secundum prius et posterius; non tamen secundum diversum esse, quia esse sanitatis non est nisi in animali. [2] *Vel secundum esse et non secundum intentionem*; et hoc contingit quando plura parificantur in intentione alicujus communis, sed illud commune non habet esse unius rationis in omnibus, sicut omnia corpora parificantur in intentione corporeitatis. Unde Logicus, qui considerat intentiones tantum, dicit, hoc nomen, corpus, de omnibus corporibus univoce praedicari: sed esse hujus naturae non est ejusdem rationis in corporibus corruptibilibus et incorruptibilibus, ut patet X Meta., text. 5, ex Philosopho et Commentatore. [3] *Vel secundum intentionem et secundum esse*; et hoc est quando neque parificatur in intentione communi, neque in esse; sicut ens dicitur de substantia et accidente; et de talibus oportet quod natura communis habeat aliquod esse in unoquoque eorum de quibus dicitur, sed differens secundum rationem majoris vel minoris perfectionis.[2] (*I Sent.* d. 19, q. 5, a. 1, ad 1m)

To the first, then, it should be replied that something is said according to analogy in three ways: [1] *according to intention alone and not according to being,* as when one intention is referred to many in an orderly way which however has being in only one of them, as the intention of health is diversely referred to animal, urine and diet in an orderly way, though not according to being, because health exists only in the animal. [2] *Or according to being and not according to intention*; this occurs when many things are made equal in some common intention that does not exist as one notion in them all, as all bodies are made equal in the intention of corporeity. Hence the dialectician who considers only intentions says that 'body' is said univocally of all bodies although the nature does not exist according to the same notion in corruptible and incorruptible bodies, as both Aristotle and Averroes make clear in the *Metaphysics.* [3] *Or according to intention and being*; this occurs when things are neither made equal in a common intention nor in being; as being is said of substance and accident. In such things the

2. St. Thomas, *In I Sent.* d. 19, q. 5, a. 2, ad 1m. *Scriptum Super Libros Sententiarum,* ed. R. P. Mandonnet, O.P. (Paris: Lethielleux, 1929), vol. 1.

common nature has some being in each of the things of which it is said, though differing according to greater and lesser perfection.

Cajetan reads this passage as providing us with a threefold division of analogous names, though he notes that the three kinds are not equally analogous names, since there is a progression from the least to the most proper.[3] Indeed, the kind he mentions first, analogy of inequality, which answers to [2] in the text just cited, is not, according to Cajetan, an analogous name at all.

Analoga secundum inaequalitatem vocantur, quorum nomen est commune, et ratio secundum illud nomen est omnino eadem, inaequaliter tamen participata. Et loquimur de inaequalitate perfectionis: ut *corpus* nomen commune est corporibus inferioribus et superioribus, et ratio omnium corporum (in quantum corpora sunt) eadem est. Quaerenti enim quid est ignis in quantum corpus, dicetur: substantia trinae dimensioni subiecta. Et similiter quaerenti: quid est caelum in quantum corpus, etc. Non tamen secundum aequalem perfectionem ratio corporeitatis est in inferioribus et superioribus corporibus. (n.4)

Those are called analogues according to inequality which have a common name and the meaning of the name is wholly the same though unequally shared. I mean inequality of perfection, as 'body' is a name common to lower and higher bodies and its meaning for all bodies (insofar as they are bodies) is the same. One asking what fire is insofar as it is a body is answered: a substance subject to three dimensions. Similarly to one asking what the heaven is insofar as it is a body, etc. However the notion signified by body is not in lower and higher bodies in an equal degree of perfection.

Cajetan does not seem to be suggesting here (n. 4) that anyone actually calls this an analogous name; indeed, logicians call the name in question univocal and philosophers say it is equivocal. Guided as he thinks by the text of Thomas, Cajetan imagines that in this sense any genus could be called an analogous term. "Omne enim genus analogum hoc modo appellari potest" (n. 5). Why? Because the differences that divide the genus are related as *habitus* and *privatio*, e.g. rational and irrational, and are ordered *per prius et posterius*. It is, Cajetan suggests, because 'to be named analo-

---

3. A question to put to Cajetan's division is this: Is this a division of a genus into its species? Presumably not. Then it is the enumeration of the analogates of the common name 'analogy'. In what sense of analogy is 'analogy' analogically common to the types. More and less proper?

gously' and 'to be named *per prius et posterius*' have become all but synonymous (n. 7) that we have this odd situation of a generic and thus univocal term being called an analogous one.

Now, if dialecticians say 'body' is predicated univocally of terrestrial and heavenly bodies but philosophers say it is predicated equivocally of them, who is it that speaks of such a term as an analogous one? It is obvious that Cajetan has in mind only the text from the *Sentences* commentary. By taking this example to stand for all generic names, Cajetan must imagine that in the case of 'animal' as in the example of 'body' there is a dialectical definition that competes with the philosophical one, but this conclusion seems doubtful in the extreme. The question must arise as to whether the *logicus* of the present text has a different conception of univocal or equivocal terms from the philosopher. Surely they agree on what such terms mean but disagree as to whether the things being talked about can provide a *ratio communis* which is found equally in them. The *logicus* here is not the logician who gives a definition of 'genus' and 'named univocally' and 'named analogically'. Rather, he is the dialectician who speaks of things, not *ex propriis,* but from the point of view of mental constructs. There is a single account, *ratio,* mental construct, answering to the term 'body'—that which has three dimensions. Taken as meaning that, 'body' is predicated univocally of terrestrial and celestial bodies. The philosopher, being interested in things themselves, sees that the terrestrial things that have three dimensions are quite unlike celestial things that have three dimensions, and, although he calls them both 'body', the fact that terrestrial bodies have a matter thanks to which they can cease to be and celestial bodies do not have such matter as a component, he, the philosopher, has in mind two accounts of 'body' that incorporate this difference. Given the plurality of *rationes,* 'body' is said equivocally of terrestrial and celestial bodies.[4]

4. "Huiusmodi autem analoga Logicus univoca appellat, Philosophus vero aequivoca, eo quod ille intentiones considerat nominum, iste autem naturas. Unde et in X *Metaph.*, text. ultm. Aristoteles dicit quod corruptibili et incorruptibili nihil est commune univocum, despiciens unitatem rationis seu conceptus tantum. Et in VII *Physic.*, text. 13 dicitur iuxta genus latere aequivocationes; quia huiusmodi analogia cum unitate conceptus non dicit unam naturam simpliciter, sed multas compatitur sub se naturas, ordinem inter se habentes, ut patet inter species cuiuslibet

Thomas's example then does not suggest several meanings of 'univocal', 'equivocal' or 'analogical' but rather calls attention to a disagreement between the dialectician and philosopher as to what constitutes one or several notions. What the dialectician calls univocal, the philosopher calls equivocal. Their disagreement is not about what 'univocal' means but about whether something exemplifies univocity.

By taking the example to be one of genus as such, Cajetan makes it even clearer that what he calls *analogia inaequalitatis* does not involve an analogous name. That man and dog, who are made equal in the notion signified by 'animal', scilicet *a living substance endowed with senses,* and thus are univocally named 'animal', does not make them equal animals. But their inequality derives from the differences which divide the genus, and, when these difference are made explicit, a new notion is formed and it is signified by the specific name, 'man', and, e.g., 'scorpion'.[5] But, unlike the example of 'body' in the text of Thomas, this leads to no dispute between dialectician and philosopher.

Whether understood as a feature of any genus or a special case exemplifying the difference between the dialectician and the philosopher, the second member of Thomas's division of things said according to analogy makes it clear that inequality *secundum esse* is irrelevant to what is meant by an analogous name, just as inequality *secundum esse* is irrelevant to the univocal character of generic terms.[6] In short, Thomas is noting that there are inequalities, orderings *per prius et posterius,* among things talked about that do

---

generis, specialissimas et subalternas magis. Omne enim genus analogum hoc modo appellari potest, (licet non multum consueverint nisi generalissima et his propinqua sic vocari), ut patet de quantitate et qualitate in praedicamentis, et corpore, etc." (*De nominum analogia,* n. 5).

5. Or, we might say that the genus animal is divided by man and beast, the latter standing for all those animals deprived of reason. Sometimes, of course, the same word is retained to signify the genus and one of the species, as we might sometime contrast man and animal within the genus of animal, using the name of the genus for the species deprived of what the more perfect species has.

6. In the *Perihermeneias,* discussing the way the enunciation is divided into affirmative and negative, Thomas speaks of *aliquod commune* divided according to the *rationes proprias* of its species. It is by the addition of the difference that the *ratio* of the specific term appropriates the genus to the species. *In I Perih.,* lectio 8, n. 6. This text is given in the next footnote.

not affect our way of talking about them. This is as true of the dialectical use of 'body'—if we simply ignore the substantive differences between the things we are talking about, differences which enter into more precise notions signified by 'body'—as it is true of any genus whose species can be ranked *per prius et posterius*.[7]

If some inequalities of the things we talk of, those *secundum esse,* do not bring about an unequal sharing of a common term, they will be irrelevant to understanding how it is that some things share a common name unequally, this inequality being a matter of the order *per prius et posterius* among notions signified by the term. Cajetan is right in seeing that Thomas here uses the phrase *secundum analogiam* to speak of inequality *secundum esse* as well as *secundum intentiones.* Only in the latter instance do we have an analogous name. However we understand Thomas's example, the former instance, inequality *secundum esse,* is not productive of an analogous name. A univocal name, one thanks to which many things are made equal in a common intention, does not preclude an inequality among the things named—not an inequality in terms of the common intention, of course, but according to the *esse hujus naturae.* Call the inequality *secundum esse* analogy and then, as Cajetan suggested, 'analogy' and 'per prius et posterius' will be the same. Of course, then, *per prius et posterius secundum esse* and *per prius et posterius secundum intentiones* will not be two kinds of analogous name, but two uses of 'analogy', the one to refer to the way a common name is shared, the other to refer to inequalities having nothing to do with shared names.

---

7. The point is made in the division of the enunciation into affirmative and negative in *In I Perih.* lectio 8, n. 6. "Sed dicendum quod unum dividentium aliquod commune potest esse prius altero *dupliciter: uno modo,* secundum proprias rationes, aut naturas dividentium; *alio modo,* secundum participationem rationis illius communis quod in ea dividitur. *Primum* autem non tollit univocationem generis, ut manifestum est in numeris, in quibus binarius secundum propriam rationem naturaliter est prior ternario; sed tamen aequaliter participant rationem generis sui, scilicet numeri: ita enim est ternarius multitudo mensurata per unum, sicut et binarius. Sed *secundum* impedit univocationem generis. Et propter hoc *ens* non potest esse genus substantiae et accidentis: quia in ipsa ratione *entis,* substantia, quae est ens per se, prioritatem habet respectu accidentis, quod est ens per aliud et in alio. Sic ergo affirmatio secundum propriam rationem prior est negatione; tamen aequalitater participant rationem enunciationis, quam supra posuit, videlicet quod enunciatio est oratio in qua verum vel falsum est."

The first member of Cajetan's threefold division of analogous names, then, is not an example of analogous name, except abusively. Cajetan provides no instance of anyone calling the genus an analogous term. Rather he is being influenced by what he takes to be the sense of the passage of Thomas, not by the use or abuse of the term elsewhere.

That is the first clue that something is radically wrong with his threefold division. But is not Cajetan justified in taking a text which begins 'aliquid dicitur secundum analogiam tripliciter' as providing three ways in which things are said according to analogy? The text, remember, is a reply to an objection. What is its point with reference to the objection it addresses?

The objector notices something about animal and medicine and urine, which are named healthy analogously, and takes it to be a necessary condition of being named analogously. Thus, if God and creature are called true analogously, the same thing must obtain among them as did among animal, medicine, and urine.

The response to the objection comes down to this. The feature *secundum esse* of things named healthy analogously is *per accidens* to their being named analogously. Other things named analogously have a different feature *secundum esse*. If some analogous names have feature X and other analogous names do not, feature X is accidental to their being analogous names. To underscore this point, Thomas notes that you can find the same variation *secundum esse* in univocal terms.

In short, the objection is based on a fallacy, and the reply points out the fallacy and rejects the conclusion drawn. What Cajetan did was to take the distinctions introduced to make this point as if they were members of a threefold division of analogous name. Missing the point of the reply, which is that different situations *secundum esse* are compatible with names being analogous, he builds those accidental differences into "types" of analogous name, a fateful move which continues to haunt Thomistic interpretation.

Cajetan, in his discussion of a generic name abusively called analogous, puts his finger on something that should have told him he was misreading the passage in Thomas. The abuse stems from identifying 'being named analogously' and 'being named per prius et posterius'. Things ordered in such a way that one is prior and the other posterior are not equal. The term 'equalized (*parificantur*)' is the key to the text. There can be inequality, a relation *per prius et posterius*, both *secundum intentionem* and *secundum esse*. The former is what is in play when we talk of a term being used analogously. Things named analogously are denominated not equally but *per prius et posterius*, unequally and with reference to one. There can be inequality and order *per prius et posterius* that is not reflected *secundum intentionem*. When the species receive the generic name, they are equalized (*parificantur*): man and beast are equally called living things endowed with senses; the one species is not denominated from the other. If the species are unequal, this is due to their specific differences, not their genus. The order *per prius et posterius* of their differences does not affect the unity and equality they enjoy thanks to their genus.

In pointing out such things, Cajetan did not realize what they mean, that, since the second member of Thomas's division and the first of his own are not analogous names, the text in Thomas is not providing us with a threefold division of analogous names. Had he recognized that, he would have written a very different opusculum, and the history of Thomistic interpretation would have been different and, presumably, accurate.

It is not simply that Cajetan got one member of Thomas's division wrong and that this can be acknowledged—the generic name is not an analogous name by any use or abuse that can be cited—and leave us with the remaining two types of analogous name Cajetan writes of. His misunderstanding of the text in the *Sentences* on which he based the *De nominum analogia,* discredits his threefold division as such. In short, there is no distinction between analogy of attribution and analogy of proportionality in St. Thomas Aquinas. It is not to be found in this text and, as we will be saying, it is equally absent elsewhere.

The point can be made schematically. Let A = an analogous name; U = a univocal name, and X an inequality among things named that does not affect the way the common name is applied. The objector says this:

a is an example of A and a has X. Therefore, b, which is A, has X.

In replying to this, Thomas says there are three situations.

1. Sometimes there is A and X.
2. Sometimes there is U and X.
3. Sometimes there is A but not X.

From this schema we would conclude that X does not affect something's being A, and this conclusion is even clearer when we note that something can be U and have X. Clearly these are not three ways of being A.

Why, then, does Thomas introduce these three accidental conjunctions with the remark that something is said according to analogy in three ways? It is already clear that he cannot be taken to mean that there are three kinds of analogous name. When analogy is used to speak of a kind of naming, there is an inequality, an order *per prius et posterius,* among the intentions it signifies. Thus, when there is inequality *secundum esse,* the term 'analogy' can be used to refer to it. Then we can say that talk of inequality can conjure up three different states of affairs (*aliquid dicitur secundum analogiam tripliciter*). Sometimes (1) there is inequality of meaning (and thus an analogous name), but the denominating quality is not multiplied in the things named so that it exists in them equally or unequally. Sometimes (2) there is inequality among things named univocally. We might put this as 'proper inequality', or 'specific inequality', or '*inaequalitas secundum rationes proprias*'. Finally, sometimes (3) there is a conjunction of order and inequality among a plurality of notions of a common term *and* unequal, more and less perfect, existence of the denominating quality in the things talked about.

It is this final state of affairs that Cajetan takes to be analogy in the most proper sense of the term, meaning that only when this situation obtains can we really and truly and properly speak of an analogous name. Here is Thomas.

Et similiter dico quod veritas et bonitas et omnia hujusmodi dicuntur analogice de Deo et creaturis. Unde oportet quod secundum suum esse omnia haec in Deo sint, et in creaturis secundum rationem majoris perfectionis et minoris; ex quo sequitur, cum non possint esse secundum unum esse utrobique, quod sint diversae veritates. (*I Sent.* d. 19, q. 5, a. 1, ad 1m)

Similarly I say that truth, goodness, and the like are said analogically of God and creatures. Hence it is necessary that all these should exist in God and in creatures according to greater and less perfection; from which it follows that, since they cannot exist numerically the same in both that there are diverse truths.

What is the upshot? The objector is wrong in arguing from accidental conjunction [1] to the denial of accidental conjunction [3]. His mistake does not lie in confusing one kind of analogous name with another, Cajetan's analogy of attribution with Cajetan's proper proportionality, but in thinking that what happens to be true of one example of analogous naming must be true of any example of analogous naming.

Cajetan as Commentator

Cajetan was the first casualty of his own misreading of the text in the *Sentences*. Later, as he comments on the parallel text in the *Summa theologiae,* his earlier opusculum gets in the way of his reading of Thomas, and he seems far more concerned to preserve his own flawed division of analogous names than to understand the text before him. Here is Thomas:

Sciendum est quod quando aliquid praedicatur univoce de multis, illud in quolibet eorum secundum propriam rationem invenitur, sicut *animal* in qualibet specie animalis. Sed quando aliquid dicitur analogice de multis, illud invenitur secundum propriam rationem in uno eorum tantum, a quo alia denominantur. Sicut *sanum* dicitur de animali et urina et medicina, non quod sanitas sit nisi in animali tantum, sed a sanitate animalis denominatur medicina sana, inquantum est illius sanitatis effectiva, et urina, inquantum est illius sanitatis signficativa. Et quamvis sanitas non sit in medicina neque in urina, tamen in utroque est aliquid per quod hoc quidem facit, illud autem significat sanitatem. (*ST,* Ia, q. 16, a. 6)

Note that when something is predicated univocally of many, it is found in each of them according to its proper notion, as 'animal' in every species of animal. But when something is said analogically of many, it is found according to its proper notion in one of them alone, from which the others are denominated. As 'healthy' is said of animal, urine and medicine, although health is only in the animal, but from the animal's health medicine is denominated healthy, insofar as it effects this health, and urine insofar as it indicates it. And although health is in neither medicine nor urine, there is, nonetheless, something in each thanks to which the one causes and the other is the sign of health.

The text asks precisely whether there is a single truth whereby all things are called true, the question of the text in the *Sentences*. Thomas approaches his solution by recalling the difference between things named univocally and things named analogously. When something is predicated univocally of many, he notes, the proper sense of the term is found in each use. When something is said analogously of many, however, it is found in its proper sense (*secundum propriam rationem*) in one alone, from which the others are denominated. Thomas rehearses the familiar example of 'healthy' and goes on to note that 'true' is said analogously of God and creature. As he makes the transition from 'healthy' to 'true', Thomas adds a cautionary note. "Although health is in neither medicine or urine, there is, nonetheless, something in each thanks to which the one causes and the other is the sign of health." We are reminded of the remarks about what may or may not obtain *secundum esse*. No one untutored would imagine that this is a further gloss on what has already been said about each and every analogous name, as if Thomas were qualifying the universal characterization of analogous terms introduced to distinguish them from univocal terms. But Cajetan comes to the text with his earlier misunderstanding weighing upon him.

VI. Ad secundum vero dubitationem dicitur, quod illa regula de analogo tradita in littera, non est universalis de omni analogiae modo: imo, proprie loquendo, ut patet in I Ethic., nulli analogo convenit, sed convenit nominibus ad unum vel in uno aut ab uno, quae nos abusive vocamus analoga. Veritas autem, si comparetur ad res et intellectus, est nomen ab uno: quoniam in intellectu solo est veritas, a qua res dicuntur verae. Si vero comparetur ad intellectus inter se, sic est nomen analogum: nam proportionaliter salvatur, formaliter tamen, in quolibet intellectu cognoscente verum. Esse ergo nomen aliquod secundum propriam rationem in uno tantum, est conditio nominum quae sunt ad unum aut ab uno, etc.: et non nominum proportionaliter dictorum. Veritas autem, respectu intellectus divini et aliorum, proportionale nomen est. Et ideo non sequitur quod in solo Deo sit. Iam enim dictum est in solutione primi dubii, quod omni praedicato formaliter de pluribus, convenit plurificari ad plurificationem subiectorum, sive illud sit univocum, ut animal, sive proportionale, ut ens, etc.—De huiusmodi autem differentia nominum plene scriptum invenies in tractatu de Analogia Nominum. (*In Iam* q. 16, a. 6)

In response to the second doubt it should be said the the rule of analogy given in the text is not true of every kind of analogy; indeed, properly speaking, as is clear from *Ethics* I, it is not true of any analogous name but only of names which are 'to one' or 'in one' or 'from one' which we abusively call analogous. Truth, however, when compared to thing and mind is a name 'from one', since truth is in mind alone, from which others are called true. If however it be compared to intellects, then it is an analogous name, for it is saved proportionally, but formally, in each mind knowing the true. Therefore, to be a name whose proper notion is in one alone, is a property of names which are 'to one' or 'from one', etc. and not of names predicated proportionally. Truth however, with respect to the divine and other minds, is a proportional name. Therefore it does not follow that it is in God alone. I already pointed out in resolving the first doubt that everything formally predicated of many is multiplied as its subjects are multiplied, whether it be a univocal term, like 'animal', or proportional, like 'being', and so forth.—You will find a complete account of the differences between such names in my treatise *On the Analogy of Names*.

How eloquent that final sentence is. See my book. Cajetan has just casually dismissed as irrelevant to truly analogous names the *regula* Thomas gives in the text. The rule applies not to analogous names, we are told, but to terms we abusively call analogous. (The 'we' here, of course, includes the author of the text on which he is commenting.) What are truly analogous terms cannot be thought of as combining what Thomas says of analogous terms in the text and a certain feature *secundum esse*. Cajetan now sees *illud invenitur secundum propriam rationem in uno tantum* as meaning just as such a certain situation *secundum esse*, one peculiar to what he has called analogy of attribution, and must accordingly deny its application to what he calls 'truly analogous terms'. Indeed, he ends by likening "truly analogous terms" and univocal terms, applying what Thomas had said of the latter to truly analogous terms. Of univocal terms Thomas had said that they are found *secundum rationem propriam* in all of the things of which they are said.

The text of St. Thomas contrasts univocal terms and analogous terms by noting that in the former the *ratio propria* is found in all the things named while in the latter it is found in only one of the things named, the others being denominated from it. Cajetan rejects this contrast, takes *ratio propria non invenitur nisi in uno* to be the denial that the *res significata* is found in all analogates, and thus ends by suggesting that, as is the case with univocal terms, when we have a truly analogous term the *ratio propria* is found in all the things named. True analogy and univocity are equated in the only feature that seems to interest Cajetan.

Let this suffice then for our indictment. Cajetan made canonical the discussion of analogy in terms of a threefold division of analogous names that is based on a fundamental misunderstanding of the point of a text in the *Sentences*. By a curious amalgamation of what is essential and what is accidental to things named analogously, he developed a notion of the truly analogous name that ends up sharing the essential feature of univocal terms. So radical is the misunderstanding that there can be no question of trying to salvage features of it, e.g., retaining the distinction between analogy of attribution and analogy of proportionality. That division is based precisely on a confusion of the essential and accidental. No more can one save Cajetan by distinguishing a logical from a metaphysical interpretation of analogy, if by this is meant that the "rule" of *ST*, Ia, q. 16, a. 6 applies to analogous names logically understood but not metaphysically understood. Cajetan's interpretation must be set aside in its totality and the texts of Thomas read afresh if we are to discover his authentic teaching.

The contrast that Cajetan draws in his commentary on *ST*, Ia, q. 16, a. 6, between truly analogous or proportional names, and those which are abusively called analogous names but should more properly be called names 'from, to, or in one', is found in his opusculum, *De nominum analogia*, as the distinction between analogy of attribution and analogy of proportionality. Although we have seen that there is no basis for the division of which these are members, given the persistent influence of the Cajetanian interpretation, it seems wise to dwell a bit on these alleged types of analogous name.

Analogy of Attribution

Analoga autem secundum attributionem sunt, quorum nomen commune est, ratio autem secundum illud nomen est eadem secundum terminum, et diversa secundum habitudines ad illum: ut *sanum* commune nomen est

medicinae, urinae et animali; et ratio omnium in quantum sana sunt, ad
unum terminum (sanitatem scilicet), diversas dicit habitudines. Si quis enim
assignet quid est animal in quantum sanum, subiectum dicet sanitatis; urinam vero in quantum sanam, signum sanitatis; medicinam autem sanitatis
proferet. Ubi clare patet, rationem sani esse nec omnino eamdem, nec omnino diversam; sed eamdem secundum quid, et diversam secundum quid,
Est enim diversitas habitudinum, et identitas termini illarum habitudinum.
(*De nominum analogia* n. 8)

Those names are analogous according to attribution which have a common
name but the meaning of that name is the same with respect to a term and
diverse with respect to relations to it: as 'healthy' is a name common to
medicine, urine and animal; and the notion of all of them insofar as they
are healthy expresses diverse relations to one term, namely, health. For if
anyone asks what animal is insofar as healthy, the answer is 'subject of
health;' urine as healthy is a sign of health, and medicine brings about
health. Hence it is clear that the notion of healthy is not in every way the
same nor wholly diverse, but the same in one respect and diverse in another.
There is diversity of relations and identity of the term of those relations.

Cajetan's definition of what he calls analogy of attribution, like
his definition of so-called analogy of inequality, mimics the definitions of things named equivocally and things named univocally with
which the *Categories* opens. The opusculum has already made clear
that Greek usage, especially Aristotelian usage, will guide Cajetan.
(In our next chapter we will discuss Aristotle and analogy and look
into Cajetan's assumption that Greek usage should control our interpretation of medieval Latin.)

In any case, it is Aristotle who suggests to Cajetan that what he
has just defined as analogy of attribution can come about in four
ways, insofar as the term to which the things named are diversely
related is a different cause: an exemplar cause (doing service for
formal causality), an efficient cause, a final cause, or one subject
(doing service as material cause). The *Metaphysics* and the *Ethics*
are the basis for this. What Cajetan does not make clear is whether
the term to which things are referred must always be a cause. That
seems to be the assumption and, if these are types of analogy of
attribution, we have here an exhaustive division.

Cajetan assigns four characteristics to analogy of attribution. It
involves extrinsic, not intrinsic denomination; that to which the
things are referred is numerically one; the primary analogate enters

into the definitions of the rest; and, it does not involve a concept which can be abstracted from the concepts of the analogates.

Extrinsic denomination is exemplified by 'healthy' as predicated of animal, medicine, and urine. Medicine and urine are denominated healthy, not from a quality intrinsic to them, but from the quality health in the animal, hence they are extrinsically denominated. Other examples are 'medical' (instruments and books denominated from the art intrinsic to the physician) and 'good'. "Boni quoque ratio in bono per essentiam salvata, quo exemplariter caetera denominantur bona, in solo primo bono formaliter invenitur; reliqua vero extrinseca denominatione, secundum illud bonum, bona dicuntur" (n. 10). This seems straightforward enough, and it matches what he said later in commenting on *ST,* Ia, q. 16, a. 6. But Cajetan adds this:

Sed diligenter advertendum est, quod haec huiusmodi analogiae conditio, scilicet quod non sit secundum genus causae formalis inhaerentis, sed semper secundum aliquid extrinsecum, est formaliter intelligenda et non materialiter: idest non est intelligendum per hoc, quod omne nomen quod est analogum per attributionem, sit commune analogatis sic, quod primo tantum conveniat formaliter, caeteris autem extrinseca denominatione, ut de sano et medicinali accidit; ista enim universalis est falsa, ut patet de ente et bono; nec potest haberi ex dictis, nisi materialiter intellectis. Sed est ex hoc intelligendum, quod omne nomen analogum per attributionem ut sic, vel in quantum sic analogum, commune est analogatis sic, quod primo convenit formaliter, reliquis autem extrinseca denominatione. (n. 11)

It must be diligently noted, however, that this mark of this type of analogy, namely that it not be according to the genus of inherent formal causality but always according to something extrinsic, must be understood formally, not materially; that is, it is not to be taken to mean that every name analogous through attribution is so common to its analogates that it belongs only to the first formally and to the others by extrinsic denomination, as happens in the case of 'healthy' and 'medicinal'. For this universal is false, as is clear from 'being' and 'good', nor does it follow unless the foregoing is understood materially. It is rather to be understood that every name analogous through attribution as such, or insofar as thus analogous, is common to its analogates thus, that it belongs to the first formally and to the others by extrinsic denomination.

When does this characteristic of analogy of attribution fail to characterize analogy of attribution? That is, what is the difference between 'being' and 'healthy'? "Although being belongs formally to all substances and accidents, etc., insofar as they are called beings they are all denominated from the being which is as subject, only substance is being formally; the others are called beings because they are properties or becomings of being, etc., although they can be called beings formally for other reasons: "Ens enim quamvis formaliter conveniat omnibus substantiis et accidentibus, etc., in quantum tamen entia omnia dicuntur ab ente subiective ut sic, sola substantia est ens formaliter; caetera autem entia dicuntur, quia entis passiones vel generationes, etc., sunt; licet entia formaliter alia ratione dici possint" (n. 11). So too with 'good'. Although all things are good by a goodness formally inherent in them, insofar as they are called good they are all denominated good extrinsically from the first efficient, final, or exemplar cause, that is, from the goodness God himself formally is.

Anyone reading this passage must be struck by the tortured language needed to defend an indefensible position. Cajetan tells us— formally, as he would say—that the differences between 'healthy' and 'being' are irrelevant to their being analogous names. It is simply not the case that they both involve extrinsic denomination. Why not just admit that 'healthy' involves extrinsic denomination and 'good' involves intrinsic denomination, and that this difference does not affect their being analogous names? In short, Cajetan is confronting another opportunity to see that his threefold division is fundamentally flawed and fails to avail himself of the chance to scrap it. His discussion of the other conditions or characteristics of "analogy of attribution" involves him in similar self-imposed difficulties.

We then learn that the mention of the four causes as terms to which relations refer was not meant to give us types of analogy of attribution. There are, we are told (n. 17) only two kinds of this analogy given by St. Thomas. (This is only the second mention of Thomas although Aristotle has been cited eight times, whether by name or text.) Analogous names involve either 'two to a third: *duorum ad tertium*' or 'one to another: *unius ad alterum*'.[8]

Cajetan remarks that what he calls analogy of attribution is called

8. *ST* Ia, q. 13, a. 5.

equivocation by the *logicus*. His reference is to the *Categories*, so that the logician is Aristotle writing the Bekker line numbers 1a1–6. Presumably, this is how Cajetan understands *logicus* in the second member of Thomas's threefold division, which has become Cajetan's analogy of inequality. 'Analogy of attribution' is explicitly linked with Thomas's first member, *secundum intentionem et non secundum esse*. He quite explicitly equates *intentio* and *denominatio* (n. 21). Greek philosophers are said to call names analogous by attribution *nomina ex uno vel ad unum aut in uno* and explicitly distinguish them from analogous names. Cajetan means Aristotle, who says "expresse in *I Ethic*. huiusmodi nomina contra analoga distinguuntur." Latins, on the other hand, call such names analogous or equivocal by design.

Speaking Greek, then, Cajetan could say that his first kind of analogous name consists of univocal names, his second of equivocal terms, and only his third of analogous names. What explains the Latins' violation of Greek usage?

Haec ideo apud Latinos analoga dicuntur: quia proportiones diversas ad unum dicunt, extenso proportionis nomine ad omnem habitudinem. Abusiva tamen locutio haec est, quamvis longe minor quam prima. (n. 21)

These are called analogous by Latins because they speak of different proportions to one, extending the word proportion to cover any relation. This is an abuse of language, however, although far less than in the first case.

It is, of course, St. Thomas Aquinas who is here being accused of a misuse of language. Why he should be held to the alleged proprieties of Greek is not explained, except perhaps on the basis that the Latin *analogia* is a loan word from the Greek. But clearly Cajetan must regard Thomas's confusion as a good deal more than terminological. For one thing, when St. Thomas wants to exemplify what he means by an analogous name, he invariably brings in 'healthy'. We have seen him do this in *ST*, Ia, q. 16, a. 6 where 'healthy' is meant to exemplify what 'true' said of God and creatures also exemplifies, that is, analogous naming. None of this makes sense on the basis of Cajetan's understanding, and that is why he wrote such an extraordinary commentary on that text. But let us see what Cajetan means by the analogous name properly understood.

Analogy of Proportionality

Cajetan continues to mimic the opening sentence of the *Categories* in defining what is properly analogy. *Analoga secundum proportionalitatem dici, quorum nomen est commune, et ratio secundum illud nomen est proportionaliter eadem*: "things are said to be analogous according to proportionality which have a common name, and the notion signified by that name is proportionally the same," or "which have a common name, and the notion signified by it is similar according to proportion" (n. 23). Since 'proportion' has been introduced as synonymous with 'analogy' (n. 21), this account could be trivialized by rephrasing it thus: "those things are said to be analogous according to analogy which have a common name, and the notion signified by the name is the same according to analogy." Cajetan gives this example: as seeing is to the eye, so seeing is to the intellect. The common term 'seeing' is understood as likening the way the mind presents something to the soul and the way sight presents something to the living body.

The terminology is taken (abusively?) from mathematics, where a proportion (or ratio) is a determined relation of one quantity to another, e.g. double as in 4:2, and a proportionality is made up of similar proportions, as in 4:2 :: 8:4. Philosophers extended the term 'proportion' to mean any relation and the term 'proportionality' to mean a similarity between relations of any kind. Earlier (n. 21), Cajetan accused the Latins of an abuse of language for extending 'analogy' to any relation, but he does not here (n. 24) chide the Greeks for doing the same thing. But there are more surprises.

Although we have now arrived at analogy properly speaking, it is subdivided into metaphorical and proper. When is analogy properly speaking improper or metaphorical?

Metaphorice quidem, quando nomen illud commune absolute unam habet rationem formalem, quae in uno analogatorum salvatur, et per metaphoram de alio dicitur: ut ridere unam secundum se rationem habet, analogum tamen metaphorice est vero risui, et prato virenti, aut fortunae successui; et sic enim significamus haec se habere, quemadmodum homo ridens. (n. 25)

Metaphorically indeed when the common name has absolutely one formal notion which is saved in one of the analogates and is said of the other by metaphor: as 'laughing' has of itself one notion but is metaphorically analogous to real laughing and to the greening field and success of fortune; for in this way we signify that they are like a man who laughs.

Cajetan disappoints us again by making metaphor essential to his definition of metaphor. A word is metaphorical when it is used metaphorically. But he has undertaken to tell us what being used metaphorically means. What we have is something extraordinarily like what he called analogy of attribution. But doubtless all obscurities are meant to fade away when we look at what analogy is in the proper sense.

Proprie vero fit, quando nomen illud commune in utroque analogatorum absque metaphoris dicitur: ut principium in corde respectu animalis, et in fundamento respectu domus salvatur. Quod, ut Averroes in comm. septimo I *Ethic*. ait, proportionaliter de eis dicitur. (n. 26)

It occurs properly when the common name is said of both analogates without metaphor, as principle is exemplified by the heart in the case of animal and by the foundation in the case of the house, which, as Averroes says in commenting on the *Ethics*, is said proportionally of them.

Proper proportionality is had when the common term is said nonmetaphorically of both analogates, that is, is said proportionally of them.

It would perhaps be unkind to draw attention to the glaring weaknesses of Cajetan's opusculum if it had not held in thrall not only its author but also countless others throughout subsequent centuries. That it is a hopelessly confused account almost from its opening page is clear enough. We want to know what analogous names are, and we are told that they are of three kinds. It emerges that the first kind is not an analogous name at all and the second is so only abusively; and, when we turn to what an analogous name is in the proper sense, we are told that it comes in two kinds, metaphorical, that is, improper, and proper. What is a metaphor? A term is used metaphorically when it is used metaphorically. What then is proper proportionality? When the common term is said nonmetaphorically of its analogates, that is, when it is said of them proportionally. This is what we have learned after looking carefully at twenty per cent of Cajetan's opusculum, and what we have learned is nothing.

Proper proportionality, whatever it is, excels in dignity what has preceded it in Cajetan's presentation, because we now learn that it comes about in the genus of formal inherent cause. Such a name predicates what it means of each of the things of which it is said. By contrast with analogy of attribution, it involves intrinsic denomination. And it is preeminent because it alone deserves to be called analogy. This claim is based on what is said to be Aristotle's usage.

Because it is not at all clear that Cajetan, in his opusculum, intends to give an account of St. Thomas's teaching on analogous naming—Thomas, after all, must be numbered among those Latins who misuse the term 'analogy'—it is important to return to the cardinal's commentary on the *Summa theologiae*.

The Divine Names

In discussing the way in which some names are common to God and creature in *ST,* Ia, q. 13, St. Thomas recalls what is meant by univocity, equivocity and analogy and then suggests that such terms as "being" and "good" and "wise" are analogically common to creatures. Cajetan's commentary on this question, typically alert to Scotist cavils, is of enormous help in understanding many difficult matters. But here, as we have already seen will be the case in his commentary on *ST,* Ia, q. 16, his own independent treatise on analogy intrudes itself between the text and its commentator. This intrusion is especially obvious in articles 5 and 6.

Thomas, having set aside the possibility that such a term as 'wise' is univocal as predicated of God and creatures, since if it were the same account (*ratio*) of the name would be given in each instance, goes on to deny that this is an equivocal use of the term, as if there were wholly different accounts given of 'wise' in "God is wise" and "Socrates is wise."

Dicendum est igitur quod huiusmodi nomina dicuntur de Deo et creaturis secundum analogiam, idest proportionem. Quod quidem dupliciter contingit in nominibus: vel quia multa habent proportionem ad unum, sicut *sanum* dicitur de medicina et urina, inquantum utrumque habet ordinem et proportionem ad sanitatem animalis, cuius hoc quidem signum est, illud vero causa; vel ex eo quod unum habet proportionem ad alterum, sicut *sanum* dicitur de medicina et animali, inquantum medicina est causa sanitatis quae est in animali. Et hoc modo aliqua dicuntur de Deo et creaturis analogice, et non aequivoce pure, neque univoce. Non enim possumus nominare Deum nisi ex creaturis, ut supra dictum est. Et sic, quidquid dicitur de Deo et creaturis, dicitur secundum quod est aliquis ordo creaturae ad Deum, ut ad principium et causam, in qua praeexistunt excellenter omnes rerum perfectiones. (*ST,* Ia, q. 13, a. 5)

It should be said therefore that names of this kind are said of God and creatures according to analogy, that is, proportion. This occurs in two ways in naming: either many things have a proportion to one, as 'healthy' is said of medicine and urine insofar as each is ordered to the health of the animal, of which the latter is the sign and the former the cause; or one is proportioned to another, as 'healthy' is said of medicine and animal, insofar as medicine is the cause of the health that is in the animal. And in this way some things are said analogically, and not purely equivocally or univocally, of God and creatures. We can name God only from creatures, as was said earlier. Thus, whatever is said of God and creatures is said insofar as there is a certain order of creature to God as to its principle and cause in which preexist in an excellent manner all the perfections in things.

We notice that St. Thomas assumes that 'healthy' can be used to exemplify the analogous name of which other examples are to be found in names common to God and creatures. Furthermore, he distinguishes two kinds of analogous name, kinds that Cajetan has assigned to what he calls "analogy of attribution" which is not truly analogy and thus cannot help us understand the point at issue in this article.

In his commentary, after summarizing the argument, Cajetan alludes to the difficulty of such univocal terms as 'body' said of terrestrial and celestial bodies (*In Iam,* q. 13, a. 5, nn. 3 and 4). He goes on to say things of remarkable pith and perception as to what Thomas can mean in the text by saying that such a term as 'wise' said of creatures signifies the perfection of wisdom as distinct from its essence, power, existence, etc. And then he turns to difficulties Scotus raised against the basic argument of the text.

As a young professor at Padua, Cajetan occupied the Thomistic chair and was expected to handle objections coming from Scotus and from the holder of the Scotist chair. The Scotist contention that 'being' is univocally common to God and creature explains the concerns of the opusculum *De nominum analogia*. As commentator on the *Summa theologiae,* responding to four Scotist difficulties, Cajetan refers to his commentary on the *De ente et essentia* as well as to the *De nominum analogia.* In the latter, he had said of "analogy of attribution" that it is a kind of equivocation, but here,in commenting on *ST,* Ia, q. 13, a. 5, noting that Thomas says names common to God and creatures are not *pure aequivoce,* 'entirely equivocal', he does not suggest that this lacks universality (n. 12). No more does he bridle at the twofold division of the text which, of course, in his opusculum he restricted to only a type of analogous name. This suggests that his opusculum is not the lens through which he reads this text, but alas that suggestion is not true.

Memento hic quod exempla ponimus, non quod ita sit, sed ut discentes intelligant. Non enim *ens* est analogum Deo et creaturis secundum denominationem extrinsecum, ut *sanum:* sed in hoc tenet similitudo, quod utrobique est analogia ratione ordinis duorum inter se, quamvis dissimiliter sit hic et ibi. Nam inter Deum et creaturam est similitudo formalis imitativa (quae etiam in littera tangitur, dum creaturas ordinari in Deum dicitur ut causam, in qua praeexistunt perfectiones omnes): inter animal vero sanum et urinam non est similitudo, sed relatio significationis. Et propterea ibi est analogica communitas secundum praedicationem formalem: hic autem proprie est communitas attributionis ad unum secundum praedicationem quamcumque, sive extrinsece sive intrinsece, etc. (n. 14)

Note that here we give examples, not as things stand, but in order that learners may understand. For 'being' is not analogous as said of God and creatures by extrinsic denomination, like 'healthy', but they are alike in this that in both there is analogy by reason of an order between the two, though differently in the two cases. For between God and creature there is a formal imitative likeness (which the text touches on in saying that creatures are said to be ordered to God as a cause in which all perfections preexist), but between the healthy animal and urine there is not a likeness but a relation of signifying. Yet in the former case there is analogy according to formal predication and in the latter case a community of attribution to one according to either extrinsic or intrinsic predication, etc.

What Cajetan says of the relation of creature to God, insofar as both are wise, and the relation between Rover and his signature in the snowbank is true enough, but it is palpable that it does not affect what is meant by an analogous name. By allowing *unius ad alterum* to travel across what in his opusculum are different kinds of analogy, Cajetan comes close to acknowledging this, as he does at the end when he mystifyingly seems to suggest that it is a matter of indifference whether denomination is intrinsic or extrinsic in "analogy of attribution." And, of course, n. 14 begins with a little caveat that suggests there is a pedagogically permissible confusion of types of analogy in the text. In n. 15, the reader is referred to *De nominum analogia*.

In commenting on article 6, Cajetan quotes Thomas against Thomas in discussing the text where he is confronted by untroubled generalizations.

> Respondeo dicendum quod in omnibus nominibus quae de pluribus analogice dicuntur, necesse est quod omnia dicantur per respectum ad unum: et ideo illud unum oportet quod ponatur in definitione omnium. Et quia ratio quam significat nomen, est definitio, ut dicitur in *IV Metaphys.*, necesse est quod illud nomen per prius dicatur de eo quod ponitur in definitione aliorum, et per posterius de aliis, secundum ordinem quo appropinquant ad illud primum vel magis vel minus: sicut *sanum* quod dicitur de animali, cadit in definitione *sani* quod dicitur de medicina . . . (*ST*, Ia, q. 13, a. 6)

I reply that it should be said that in all names that are said of many analogically it is necessary that all are said with respect to one, and therefore that that one must enter into the definition of all. And because the notion the name signifies is a definition, as is said in the *Metaphysics*, it is necessary that the name be said first of that which enters into the definition of the others, and secondarily of the others according to the order in which they more or less approximate the first, as 'healthy' as said of animal enters into the definition of 'healthy' said of medicine . . .

A more deontological passage could scarcely be imagined; gerundives vie with *oportet*'s and *necesse*'s. The reader gets the impression that, when St. Thomas says that these things are true of all analogous names, he means just that. Cajetan raises two difficulties. First, in *Quaestio Disputata de veritate*, q. 2, a. 11, Thomas seems to deny that it is always true that the primary analogate enters into the definitions of secondary analogates. Second, it does not seem true that divine wisdom enters into the account of human wisdom or vice versa (n. 3).

> Ad hoc breviter dicitur, quod analoga inveniuntur duobus modis. Quaedam enim significant *ipsos respectus* ad primum analogatum, ut patet de *sano*. Quaedam vero signficant *fundamenta* tantum illorum respectuum; ut com-

muniter invenitur in omnibus vere analogis, proprie et formaliter salvatis in omnibus analogatis. Propositio ergo illa universalis in antecedente assumpta, intelligenda est universaliter in primo modo analogiae: ita quod sensus est, quod in omnibus nominibus quae de pluribus analogice, idest secundum diversos respectus, dicuntur, oportet poni unum. In quaestione *de Veritate,* de secundo modo analogiae dixit oppositum. Et haec responsio est universalior ea quam alibi assignavimus, ex *Qu. de Ver.,* quia ista responsio habet locum etiam in analogis secundum proportionalitatem, metaphorice tamen dictis: in his enim etiam unum ponitur in ratione alterius. (n. 4)

To this it can be said, briefly, that analogous names are of two kinds. For some signify the relations themselves to the primary analogate, as in 'healthy'. But others signify only the bases of those relations, as is commonly the case in all true analogues, properly and formally saved in all analogates. Therefore that universal proposition assumed in the antecedent must be understood universally of the first kind of analogy, so that its sense is that in all names said of many analogically, that is, according to diverse relations, it is necessary to posit one. In *On Truth* he says the opposite, speaking of the second kind of analogy. This is a more comprehensive response than that I gave elsewhere, on the basis of *On Truth,* because this response also covers metaphorical analogies according to proportionality, in which one is also put in the definition of the other . . .

Cajetan's assignment of the universal claim about analogous terms to some analogous names, to all of which the claim applies, is guided by his assumption that there are other kinds of analogous name. Nothing in the text of Thomas suggests that; much in the text provided Cajetan the opportunity to rethink the doctrine of his early opusculum. But even when he seems to disagree with the *De nominum analogia,* as in the instances mentioned a little earlier, there is no disposition to see that his threefold division of analogous names is colliding with the text and, far from illuminating it, is obfuscating it.

It is unnecessary to say that these criticisms of Cajetan bear on quite specific points and are not part of any wholesale dismissal of the great commentator. That Cajetan often permits Scotist problematics to guide his presentation of Thomas is well known, and it is often necessary to take this into account to understand why he is taking up the questions he does. The problem with Cajetan's doctrine of analogy is almost unique. As a young man of 29 he wrote a brief treatise on a vexed topic. Unfortunately, his approach to analogous names is governed by his misunderstanding of *I Sent.* d. 19, q. 5, a. 2, ad 1m. Although, from the very outset of the *De nominum analogia,* he is plagued with difficulties because of his misbegotten threefold distinction, he seems never, then or later, to have questioned his understanding of Thomas's text. In any case, Cajetan's teaching on analogy and its effect on his interpretation of the *Summa theologiae* is a special, even unique, instance and in no wise characterizes his magnificent commentary.

TWO

ANALOGY IN ARISTOTLE

The working assumption of the *De nominum analogia* is that, since the Latin word *analogia* is borrowed from the Greek, it is Greek usage that is regulative. This assumption is clear from the way Cajetan speaks of the Latin use of the word as abusive, indeed as involving degrees of gaucherie, insofar as it departs more or less from the Greek. Whatever one might say of this as a principle of interpretation, it is only in its narrower implications that it interests us here. No great violence would be done to Cajetan's opusculum if we were to substitute "Aristotle" whenever he speaks of the Greeks. It is Aristotelian usage that is normative for Cajetan. How does this assumption affect our understanding of St. Thomas?

Like his master Thomas, Cajetan held Aristotle in the highest esteem, and there is certainly nothing controversial about seeing Thomas as, at bottom, an Aristotelian. What is controversial, however, is the assumption that there is a one-to-one correspondence between Aristotle's use of the Greek *analogia*, and its cognates, and Thomas's use of the Latin *analogia, analogice, secundum analogiam*, etc. That Cajetan makes this assumption is clear from the way he chides Latin writers for departing from Aristotelian usage, a charge that must include St. Thomas himself.

Cajetan is fully aware that oftentimes, when Thomas comments on Aristotle or simply refers to him, he speaks of analogous names when there is no occurrence of the Greek counterpart in the Aristotelian text despite the fact that the Latin is a loan word from the Greek. Cajetan's unfortunate assumption is that the texts in which Aristotle does speak of analogy should control our interpretation of the Thomistic passages where we find Thomas speaking of analogy, although *analogia* does not occur in the Aristotelian text being commented upon.

Since our interest is to clarify what St. Thomas means by analogous names, we will examine some key passages in his Aristotelian commentaries in which he speaks of analogy where Aristotle has not. We will then look at some passages in Aristotle where analogy is discussed and ask if what is said is relevant to what Thomas means by analogous *names*. Our contention will be that the Thomistic doctrine of analogous names has its counterpart in Aristotle, though not in that terminology, and that Aristotle's doctrine of analogy, when he is using that term and its cognates, is not identical with the Thomistic doctrine of analogous names.

Without Counterpart in Aristotle

a. Physics *III, 200b32–201a3.*   In Book III of the *Physics* (200b32–201a3), Aristotle turns to the study of motion or change and enumerates various kinds of it: substantial change, locomotion, quantitative change and qualitative change. "It is always with respect to substance or to quantity or to quality or to place that what changes changes. But it is impossible, as we assert, to find anything *common* to these that is neither 'this' nor *quantum* nor *quale* nor any of the other predicates. Hence neither will motion and change have reference to something over and above the things mentioned, for there *is* nothing over and above them." In commenting on this, Thomas says:

His autem generibus non est accipere aliquod commune univocum, quod non contineatur sub aliquo praedicamento, quod sit genus eorum: sed ens est commune ad ea secundum analogiam, ut in IV *Metaphys.* ostendetur. (lectio 1, n. 7)

Nothing can be found that is common to these kinds which would be their genus and univocal; that which is common to them is not contained under a certain category: but being is common to them according to analogy, as is shown in *Metaphysics* IV.

Change is not such a genus that the kinds of change coming under it are its species. If it were, 'change' would be predicated univocally of them. Thomas adds that 'being' is predicated of the categories in which change falls, but that it is analogously common to them. What interests us is the fact that Thomas refers to *Metaphysics* IV for textual grounding of the point.

b. Metaphysics *IV, 2, 1003a33–b16.*   Clearly Thomas is thinking of Chapter Two of the Fourth Book where Aristotle addresses the following problem. How can there be, over and above natural science and mathematics, a science of being as being if being is not a genus? That being is not a genus is a truth developed in Book Three.[1] How can one science treat of substance and accident when there is no genus that contains them? The question makes sense only against the background of the logic of demonstration developed in the *Posterior Analytics*. The subject of the science (*genus subiectum*) is univocally common to subjects of the demonstrations which fall under it.[2] What is the solution?

Quaecumque communiter unius recipiunt praedicationem, licet non univoce, sed analogice de his praedicetur, pertinent ad unius scientiae considerationem: sed ens hoc modo praedicatur de omnibus entibus: ergo omnia entia pertinent ad considerationem unius scientiae, quae considerat ens inquantum ens, scilicet tam substantias quam accidentia. (lect. 1, n. 534)

Whatever have some one thing commonly predicated of them, even though not univocally, it being predicated of them analogically, fall to one science; but being is predicated in this way of all beings; therefore all beings fall to the consideration of one science, which considers being as being, namely both substances and accidents.

---

1. Cf. Thomas, *In III Metaphysic.*, lect. 8, n. 433. The text in Aristotle is 998b22–27.

2. The *genus subiectum* is that which generates the properties predicated of it in the conclusion of a demonstration. Insofar as that subject matter, e.g. continuous quantity, is common to plane and solid figure, and plane figure common to rectangles and triangles and circles, the community and genus involved is predicable and univocal. How then can things fall to the same science which do not come under a common genus?

In his commentary on the *Physics,* Thomas referred to the *Metaphysics* for the proof that being is analogically common to substance and accident. We find exactly this sort of talk in his commentary on *Metaphysics* IV, 2, but we do not find the corresponding Greek expression in the text of Aristotle.

"There are many senses in which a thing may be said 'to be', but all that 'is' is related to one central point, one definite kind of thing, and is not said to 'be' by a mere ambiguity."[3] Aristotle gives as examples of the sort of thing he means 'healthy' and 'medical'.

Everything which is healthy is related to health, one thing in the sense that it produces it, another in the sense that it is a symptom of health, another because it is capable of it. And that which is medical is relative to the medical art, one thing being called medical because it possesses it, another because it is naturally adapted to it, another because it is a function of the medical art. And we shall find many other words used similarly to these. (*Metaphysics* IV, 2, 1003a35–1003b4)

If we understand how 'healthy' and 'medical' are common to diverse things, we will then be able to see how 'being' is common to whatever is said to be. Nowhere in the Aristotelian text is there any employment of ἀναλογία in the nominative or dative nor do we find the phrase κατ' ἀναλογίαν. Are we to take this to be a linguistic *faux pas* on Thomas's part, an abuse of language, because he does not conform his Latin to the Greek on which he is commenting? Certainly, on the basis of these texts, we would have to say that where Thomas is talking of analogous names, names analogously common to many, Aristotle speaks of things said in many ways, with reference to one and the same nature, and not equivocally. Rather than chide Thomas, we should perhaps draw some such conclusion as the following. When Thomas speaks of analogous names he does not mean to echo a linguistic expression of Aristotle's, since in the texts which occasion talk of analogous names in Thomas's commentary Aristotle uses such phrases as 'said in many ways with reference to one'. Aristotle clearly means to contrast that kind of talk with univocally common and equivocally common terms. Thus, *what* Thomas and Aristotle are both talking about is the same, but they do not *label*

3. This is the Oxford translation of *Metaphysics* IV, 2, 1003a33–34: τὸ δ' ὂν λέγεται μὲν πολλαχῶς, ἀλλὰ πρὸς ἓν καὶ μίαν τινὰ φύσιν, καὶ οὐχ ὁμωνύμως.

it in the same way. There is no fixed relation between Aristotle's use of the Greek term and Thomas's use of the Latin loan-word.

This conclusion, of course, will seem like a pretty quick generalization on the basis of one text, and so it would be if that text were rare. But such identity of doctrine and difference of terminology is found again and again when we compare Thomistic commentary and Aristotelian text.

c. Metaphysics V.   Sometimes Thomas uses a phrase rather than the adverb *analogice* or other variation on the stem. He does this at the outset of his commentary on *Metaphysics* V when he is about to discuss the list of words Aristotle drew up as of particular interest to the metaphysician, since they relate to the subject, properties, or principles of his science.

Et quia ea quae in hac scientia considerantur, sunt omnibus communia, nec dicuntur univoce, sed secundum prius et posterius de diversis, ut in quarto libro est habitum; ideo prius distinguit intentiones nominum, quae in huius scientiae consideratione cadunt. (lect. 1, n. 749)

Because the things considered in this science are common to all, yet are not said univocally but rather in an orderly fashion about diverse things, as was shown in Book Four, he first distinguishes the meanings of the names which fall to the consideration of this science.

It is clear that for Thomas *dicitur de diversis secundum prius et posterius* is equivalent to *dicitur analogice de diversis*. What he says of the one or the other is what Aristotle says of things said in many ways with reference to one common nature and not equivocally. The correlation was made in Book Four, to which he here refers.

d. Metaphysics VII, 4, 1030a16–27.   This correlation can also be seen in Thomas's commentary on *Metaphysics* VII, 4, 1030a16–27 (= Thomas, lect. 4, nn.1334–1337). Aristotle is pointing out that essence and definition do not have the same sense in the cases of substance and accident but neither are they used equivocally. How then? Well, πλεοναχῶς, which the Latin renders *multipliciter dicitur*. Only substance has a *what*, is something that exists *per se*. If the definition expresses quiddity or whatness, it looks as if only substances can be defined. Aristotle, having first explored the option that substances alone have essences and they alone are defined, goes on to allow that, in a sense, accidents have an essence and can be defined, just as in a sense secondary to and relative to substance accidents can be said to be. "What is whiteness?" "Color." That looks a lot like "What is man?" and the answer, "animal." Although color may be said to be what whiteness is, whiteness is not a thing that exists in and of itself. "Its what," Thomas writes, "is more *like* substance than really substance: *Et hoc quid, magis est substantiale quam substantia*" (n. 1333).[4]

It is not simply by inference that my point can be made, however. Thomas here links *multipliciter dicitur* to Book Four where he had offered *analogice dicitur* as a synonym of *multipliciter dicitur*. The identification is made again in the commentary on this passage of Book Seven. Quiddity (essence) and definition are not predicated univocally of substance and accidents, but neither are they predicated of them altogether equivocally (*omnino aequivoce*) (n. 1337). Why not? "In things spoken of equivocally there is no reference to one: *cum in aequivocis non habeatur respectus ad aliquod unum*." (ibid.) How then? "Well, it is said analogically with respect to one: *sed dicitur analogice per respectum ad unum . . .*" (ibid.)

Although our present interest is simply to establish the non-correlation of Aristotelian and Thomistic usage, it may be well to notice here remarks made about analogous naming.

a. It is linked with participation: "Therefore substance's mode of being, namely to be some thing, is participated by way of similarity of proportion in all other categories (*ideo modus entitatis substantiae, scilicet esse quid,* PARTICIPATUR *secundum quamdam similitudinem proportionis in omnibus aliis praedicamentis* (n. 1333).

b. It is linked with proportional similarity (*similitudo propor-*

---

4. Thomas spells out this idea in an interesting passage: "Propter hoc enim quod omnia alia praedicamenta habent rationem entis a substantia, ideo modus entitatis substantiae, scilicet esse quid, participatur secundum quamdam similitudinem proportionis in omnibus aliis praedicamentis; ut dicimus, quod sicut animal est quid hominis, ita color albedinis, et numerus dualitatis; et ita dicimus qualitatem habere quid non simpliciter, sed huius. Sicut aliqui dicunt logice de non ente loquentes, non ens est, non quia non ens sit ens simpliciter, sed quia non ens est non ens. Et simpliciter qualitas non habet quid simpliciter, sed quid qualitatis" (ibid., n. 1334). It is clear that *similitudo proportionis* is introduced to explain the *proportio ad unum*.

tionis) in the same passage, as we have already noted. The sequel of the text invites spelling out the similar proportions:

animal :	*color* :	*number*
man	whiteness	duality

c. Analogous predication involves a common name whose accounts look like the adding or taking away of certain features, such that the word applies more or less to the different things to which it is applied, that is, according to an order of primary and secondary application.[5]

All of these statements are said to be exemplified in the way 'being' is said of many things, of substance and accidents, even of being as 'what is the case' and of non-being. But 'being' itself is usually approached by way of other less philosophically charged examples, namely, 'healthy' and 'medical'. 'Medical' is common to things called medical, by *reference* to one and the same thing, but not as *meaning* one and the same thing; that is, not all get the same account, *ratio* or *logos*. Such terms, Thomas notes, fall midway between univocal and equivocal terms and are called analogous. There is no occurrence of the corresponding Greek term in the Aristotelian passage being explained.

Once more, it may seem quixotic in criticizing Cajetan to be insisting on a point of which the great cardinal was surely aware. It would not come as news to him that there is a non identity of Latin and Greek usage when such common terms as 'healthy' and 'medical' are under discussion. But Cajetan takes this to be a sign of the sloppiness of Latin. Such names *de facto* are called, but *de iure* ought not to be called, analogous, because the Greeks, i.e. Aristotle, did not call them analogous. But of course in his opusculum Cajetan was interested in talking about *analogous names*. He insists that only those names are truly analogous that Aristotle called analogous names. We must, therefore, look at those passages in Aristotle—or at least a representative sample of them—that should, according to Cajetan, have set the standard for Latin talk of analogous names.

5. "Manifestum est enim quod oportet definitionem et quod quid est vel aequivoce praedicari in substantia et accidentibus, vel addentes et auferentes secundum magis et minus, sive secundum prius et posterius, ut ens dicitur de substantia et accidente" (ibid., n. 1335).

Ἀναλογία in Aristotle

Despite the discrepancy between the Aristotelian and Thomistic vocabularies, Aristotle was long read as if he used the Greek ἀναλογία in exactly the same way that Thomas employs the Latin loan word. There seems little doubt that this is due to the influence of Cajetan. For example, G. L. Muskens makes Aristotle sound not just like Thomas but like Cardinal Cajetan, employing the full panoply of the threefold distinction of analogy which forms the basis of the *De nominum analogia.*[6]

Father Ramirez, in his multi-volume *De Analogia,* seems driven by the assumption that, whether in the original Greek or borrowed in other languages, 'analogy' has a unified history from antiquity to the present. He sees no conflict between Thomas's usage and Aristotle's.[7]

In VII Metaphysic., *lect. 2, n. 1276.*   In Book Seven, when he sets out to discuss substance, Aristotle mentions four things the term is commonly taken to mean: the essence, the universal, the genus, and finally the subject of which everything is predicated. Thomas has interesting things to say about the relation between this enumeration and that in the *Categories.* What is predicated of the subject are genera, species and differences as well as common and proper accidents. He exemplifies this with Socrates. "Although man, animal, rational, risible, and white are said of Socrates, he, the subject, is not predicated of them. This should be understood *per se,* since nothing prevents Socrates from being predicated *per accidens* of this white, or animal, or man, since that in which white, animal, and man are is Socrates. The subject is predicated *per se* of itself, as in 'Socrates is Socrates'. Clearly what is here called subject is in the *Categories* named first substance; the same definition is assigned to subject here and to first substance there" (n. 1273). Is it possible to collapse the fourfold division of the *Metaphysics* into

---

6. G. L. Muskens, *De vocis analogiae significatione ac usu apud Aristotelem* (Groningen: Wolters, 1943).

7. Santiago Maria Ramirez, O.P., *De Analogia,* ed. Victorino Rodriguez (Madrid: Instituto de Filosofia "Luis Vives," 1970).

the twofold division of the *Categories*? The obstacle to this lies in the non-occurrence of essence or quiddity in the latter, and its prominence in the former.

Unde patet quod fere eadem est divisio substantiae hic posita, cum illa quae ponitur in *Praedicamentis.* Nam per subiectum intelligitur hic substantia prima. Quod autem dixit genus et universale, quod videtur ad genus et species pertinere, continetur sub substantiis secundis. Hoc autem quod quid erat esse hic ponitur, sed ibi praetermittitur, quia non cadit in praedicamentorum ordine nisi sicut principium. Neque enim est genus neque species neque individuum, sed horum omnium formale principium. (n. 1275)

The division of substance given here is clearly almost identical with that given in the *Categories,* since by 'subject' is understood here first substance. What he says of genus and universal, which seem to mean genus and species, places them under second substance. Here he mentions the essence whereas there it is omitted because it does not fall within the order of the categories save as a principle. It is neither genus nor species nor individual, but the formal principle of them all.

We are, of course, reminded of what is said of the 'nature absolutely considered' in the *De ente et essentia,* and this passage will support what we say later about Thomas's conception of the nature of logic. At present we are interested in the way Thomas expresses Aristotle's next point, which is that the subject is sometimes matter, sometimes form, sometimes the composite of these. Although there is no linguistic reason in the text of Aristotle for him to do so, Thomas observes that this threefold division of 'subject' is productive of an analogous term.

Dicit ergo primo quod subiectum, quod est prima substantia particularis, in tria dividitur, scilicet in materiam, et formam, et compositum ex eis. Quae quidem divisio non est generis in species, sed alicuius analogice praedicati, quod de eis, quae sub eo continentur, per prius et posterius praedicatur. Tam quia compositum quam materia et forma particularis substantia dicitur, sed non eodem ordine; et ideo posterius inquiret quid horum per prius sit substantia. (n. 1276)

First he says that the subject, which is first particular substance, is divided into three: matter, form and the composite of these. This division is not that of a genus into its species, but of something that is analogically predicated—i.e. of one first, another after—of those things contained under it. Both the composite and the matter and particular form are called substance, but not in the same order, which is why later he will ask which of these is substance primarily.

The passage is also interesting because it goes on to speak of a metaphorical usage:

Exemplificat autem hic membra in artificialibus, in quibus aes est ut materia, figura ut 'forma speciei', idest dans speciem, statua compositum ex his. Quae quidem exemplificatio non est accipienda secundum veritatem, sed secundum similitudinem proportionis. Figura enim et aliae formae artificiales non sunt substantiae, sed accidentia quaedam. Sed quia hoc modo se habet figura ad aes in artificialibus, sicut forma substantialis ad materiam in naturalibus, pro tanto utitur hoc exemplo, ut demonstrat ignotum per manifestum. (n. 1277)

He exemplifies these members [of the division] here with an artifact, in which bronze is as matter, shape as the 'form of a species', that is, giving the species, and the statue the composite of these. This example should not be taken literally but as a proportional similarity. Shape and other artificial forms are not substances, but accidents. But because in the artifact shape is to bronze as substantial form to matter in natural things, he uses this example simply in order to demonstrate the unknown through what is manifest.

Focal Meaning and Analogy

But first let us consider an influential argument of G. E. L. Owen.[8] Owen argues that, although Aristotle had from early on become aware of the sort of thing he exemplifies with 'medical' and 'healthy', it did not stop him from making fun of the Platonic talk of an Idea of the Good. So too Aristotle dismisses, Owen holds, any science of being. In both cases, the terms range over such a variety of things that it is impossible to come up with a single universal notion that would cover all the uses. There are irreducibly different ways of being—to be is to be something or other—and we have to take them up one at a time. In any case, Owen sees this as a rejection of a science of being as such.

When, in the Fourth Book of the *Metaphysics,* Aristotle says unflinchingly that "there is a science of being as being and of that

---

8. G. E. L. Owen, "Logic and Metaphysics in Some Earlier Works of Aristotle." In *Logic, Science and Dialectic: Collected Papers in Greek Philosophy,* edited by Martha Nussbaum (Ithaca: Cornell University Press, 1986), pp. 180–199.

which belongs to it per se," Owen sees it as a rejection of the earlier view. Aristotle was able to change his mind, not so much by discovering what Owen calls *focal meaning*, but rather by seeing the applicability of this account to the many senses of 'being'.

The new treatment of τὸ ὄν and other cognate expressions as πρὸς ἓν καὶ μίαν φύσιν λεγόμενα, 'said relative to one thing and to a single character'—or as I shall henceforth say, as having *focal meaning*—has enabled Aristotle to convert a special science of substance into the universal science of being, 'universal just inasmuch as it is primary'.[9]

A word has focal meaning when there are various definitions answering to it "but one of these senses is primary, in that its definition reappears as a component in each of the other definitions."[10] As early as the *Eudemian Ethics*[11], Aristotle had seen focal meaning as a way of handling the different uses of a term like 'medical'. A man is 'medical' if he possesses the art of healing, a knife is medical if it is useful for a man having the art of healing (1236a7–33). 'Medical' is not predicated of the physician and the instrument univocally— there is no single account which serves in the two cases—nor is it equivocal—the dependence of the meaning 'medical' has when said of the instrument on the meaning it has when said of the physician precludes that. It is this familiar Aristotelian analysis which, when applied to 'being', sweeps away his objections to a general science as we find them in, say, the *Nicomachean Ethics*.

What Owen calls focal meaning—a common predicate's having different but connected definitions in its different uses, the connection being provided by its primary sense on which the others depend—answers to what Thomas Aquinas calls an analogous name. Although Owen makes no mention of analogy in explicating either focal meaning or its application in *Metaphysics* IV, he relates this

---

9. Ibid., p. 184 (= 169 of original publication *Aristotle and Plato in the Mid-Fourth Century*, ed. I. During and G. E. L. Owen, Papers of the Symposium Aristotelicum [Goteborg: Elanders Boktryckerie Aktibolag, 1960]).

10. Ibid.

11. I say 'early' because Owen's article is haunted by the problem of the chronology of Aristotle's works that still characterizes Aristotelian studies. Not that chronology is extrinsic to his argument. Assuming that Aristotle had grasped the notion of 'focal meaning' at a time when he resolutely opposed a general science, Owen takes the use of focal meaning to explain the possibility of a general science in *Metaphysics* IV.2, as a later realization.

passage to others where Aristotle does make use of *analogia*. Since the *Nicomachean Ethics* had derided the Platonic effort to have a single science of the good, suggesting that it is as impossible as a single science of being, whereas *Metaphysics IV* asserts that there is a science of being as being, Owen naturally compares the two texts.

What precisely does Aristotle say in the *Nicomachean Ethics*? The term 'good' is used in the category of substance and of quantity and of relation and cannot therefore be something universally present in all cases and single, for then it would be predicated in only one category, not all. "Further, since of the things answering to one Idea there is one science, there would have been one science of all the goods; but as it is there are many sciences even of what falls under one category . . ." (1096a30–32).

But what then do we mean by the good? It is surely not like the things that only chance to have the same name. Are goods one, then, by being derived from one good or by all contributing to one good, or are they rather one by analogy? Clearly as sight is in the body, so reason is in the soul, and so on in other cases. (1096b27–29)

Annoyingly, Aristotle stops and dismisses the subject as belonging more appropriately to another branch of philosophy. Commentators have taken this to be a reference to the resolution of *Metaphysics*, IV.2. The sequel in the *Ethics* makes it clear that Aristotle does not think the content of the passage just quoted underwrites the possibility of a single science of either the good or of being. But in both the *Eudemian Ethics* (1218a1–15) and the *Nicomachean Ethics* (1096a17–23), Aristotle recognizes different senses of 'good' as it is used in different categories, "but also a general order of *priority* among different types of good." This would tell against Owen, if the types of good recognized correspond to the senses of 'good', and if the priority in question is that of the first category.

Owen challenges this view by distinguishing the priority recognized there by Aristotle from the priority which alleges an ambiguity and exploits the theory of the categories. In short, Owen distinguishes priority in *logos* or definition from natural priority. Logical priority is exemplified by the way in which the focal meaning is presupposed by other senses of a common predicate. Real priority is shown by the fact that A can exist without B, but not *vice versa*. The sole kind of priority in play in the *Ethics* is natural priority, and focal meaning and the related notion of logical priority are left unconsidered.[12]

Owen gives no special attention to the occurrence of *kat'analogian* in the passage of the *Nicomachean Ethics*. He can scarcely avoid it, however, when he compares *Metaphysics* IV and XII, 4, 1070b10–21, where we read that all things have the same elements 'by analogy'. Surely this passage is parallel to IV.2 and, whatever the fate of Owen's argument, it is certainly relevant to our own. *Metaphysics* XII, 4 stands athwart the effort to show that there is nothing in Aristotle's use of the Greek *analogia* that answers to Thomas's use of the loan word to speak of analogous names. Owen's own judgment is precise. "But now it is time to take up an earlier promise and show that these two pronouncements, in IV and XII respectively, are by no means equivalent, despite the immemorial tendency of commentators to describe the theory in IV as 'the analogy of being'."[13] How does he show this?

First, he claims that to say that 'being' has focal meaning is "a claim that statements about non-substances can be reduced to—translated into—statements about substances; and it seems to be a corollary of this claim that non-substances cannot have matter or form of their own since they are no more than the logical shadows of substance (1044b8–11).

To say of being that it has focal meaning is to say that to call non-substances beings is unpacked by referring to what is meant by saying substance is being. A seeming corollary of this statement, Owen suggests, is that non-substances called being do not have matter and form of their own, since they are components of substance. The *Metaphysics* XII formulation in terms of analogy implies no such reduction of non-substance to substance, and this leaves Aristotle free to say that matter, form, and privation are not confined to the first category (1070b19–21).

To establish a case of focal meaning is to show a particular connexion between the definitions of a polychrestic word. To find an analogy, whether between the uses of such a word or anything else, is not to engage in any

12. Ibid., pp. 185–186 (= 170–172).
13. Ibid., p. 192 (= 180).

such analysis of meanings: it is merely to arrange certain terms in a (supposedly) self-evident scheme of proportion. So when Aristotle says in *Metaphysics* XII that the elements of all things are the same by analogy, the priority that he ascribes to substance is only a natural priority (1071a35) and he does not recognize any general science of being *qua* being. There is no mention of *pros hen legomena* in XII, and none of analogy in IV.[14]

If this contrast can be generalized—and Owen gives it a generalized form in the passage quoted—we could conclude (1) that what Aristotle calls πρὸς ἕν λεγόμενα, or words that πολλαχῶς λεγόμενα, he never calls instances of analogy. Thus, since Thomas calls such words analogous terms, he uses the loan word analogy as Aristotle never uses it in its native language. Furthermore (2), the priority of the focal meaning in a term having other meanings parasitic on it is a logical not a natural priority, whereas the priority of things related by analogy is a natural one. Indeed, Owen cites *Metaphysics* 1077a36–b11 as a place where Aristotle insists that logical priority does not entail natural priority.[15] No wonder Owen shows impatience with those commentators who confuse what Aristotle says about analogy with what he says about words having focal meaning. Since Thomas, writing in Latin, employed the phrase *analogice dicuntur* as synonymous with πολλαχῶς λεγόμενα, he unwittingly provided commentators like Cajetan and much later Muskens with occasion to conflate two considerations as different as the logical and real orders are different. Thomas himself, however, was never guilty of the confusion.

G. E. L. Owen refers to 'commentators' but his chief concern is to argue for a correct understanding of Aristotle, an understanding that requires that we distinguish between what Aristotle calls analogy and what he calls words of focal meaning. That the latter are what Thomas Aquinas means by analogous names does not enter into Owen's landmark essay. Enrico Berti, writing a quarter of a century after Owen, contrasts Aristotle's and Thomas's use of the term analogy and its cognates.[16] But Berti, like other recent

14. Ibid. pp. 192–193 (= 180–181).
15. Ibid. p. 186 (= 172), note 19. He refers to 1081b34–37 for reinforcement.
16. Enrico Berti, "L'Analogia dell'Essere nella Tradizione Aristotelico-Tomistica,"

writers on the role that analogy plays in the thought of Aristotle, proceeds within the ambience of the presumed position of St. Thomas. That is, the division of analogy set forth by Cajetan is accepted as good money, and then such questions as the following arise:

Do we find both analogy of attribution and analogy of proportionality in Aristotle?
Which of these takes pride of place?
Do we find the analogy of being in Aristotle, or is it rather of Neoplatonic origin?
And so on.[17]

By the 'analogy of being' is meant a hierarchical conception of the universe, whereby accidents depend on substance, material substances on immaterial, and immaterial substances finally on God. The hierarchy is characterized by the lower participating in the higher and the higher functioning as the ideal of which the lower is a defective imitation. The question then becomes: Does what Aristotle call equivocation *pros hen* exhibit the characteristics of the analogy of being? Here, again, opinions divide.[18]

Berti does not question whether Thomas Aquinas ever spoke of analogy of attribution and/or analogy of proportionality, but simply uses this Cajetanian frame for his discussion of the issue. If the argument of the previous chapter is sound, this procedure is unlikely

---

Metafore dell'invisibile, Ricerche sull'analogia, Contributi al XXXIII Convegno del Centro di Studi filosofici di Gallarate (Brescia: Morcelliana, 1984), pp. 13–33; "L'Analogia in Aristotele: Interpretazioni Recenti e Possibili Sviluppi," *Origini e Sviluppi dell'Analogia Da Paremenide a S. Tommaso*, a cura di Giuseppe Casetta (Rome: Edizioni Vallombrosa, 1987), pp. 94–115.

17. Berti provides a good guide into recent literature. See "L'analogia dell'essere nella tradizione aristotelico-tomistica," pp. 13–33, and "L'Analogia in Aristotele." Pierre Aubenque argues that there is no 'analogy of being' in Aristotle. Cf. "Néoplatonisme et l'analogie de l'être," in *Néoplatonisme: Mélanges offerts à J. Trouillard* (Fontenay aux Roses, 1981), pp. 63–76. Joseph Moreau, on the other hand, finds the analogy of being in Aristotle See "La Tradizione Aristotelica e l'*Analogia Entis*," in *Metafore dell'invisibile*, pp. 91–96.

18. Wilfried Fiedler's *Analogiemodelle bei Aristoteles: Untersuchungen zu den Vergleichen zwischen den einselnen Wissenschaften und Kunsten* (Amsterdam: Gruner, 1978) is a work of great importance for analogy as a form of argument in Aristotle. Fiedler alludes to G. E. L. Owen, Joseph Owens and others interested in our problem, but it is not Fielder's own.

to lead to a useful comparison of Aristotle and Aquinas on the matter of analogy.[19]

If we do consider the great historical sweep that Berti rightly takes to be a fact, however, and of course it cannot be ignored, there is no doubt that the discussion of analogy has been controlled by the Cajetanian division.[20] And that tradition retains its interest and importance even if, as is being argued here, it is founded on a faulty reading of Aquinas yet asserts that Aristotelian usage is regulative of proper talk about analogy. The previous chapter attempted to show that Cajetan has got Thomas wrong; the present chapter argues that he has got Aristotle wrong as well. Indeed, recent discussions can be seen as efforts to escape from the Cajetanian framework in order to engage Aristotle more directly.

We have seen how often Thomas will speak of analogous names when there is no occurrence of *analogia* in the Aristotelian text on

19. In fairness to Berti, it should be noticed that he is speaking of the Aristotelian-Thomistic tradition. Moreover, he provides a definition of what he means by that tradition. "Quest'ultima espressione non vuole presuppore alcuna unità fra il pensiero di Aristotele e quello di san Tommaso d'Aquino, ma si riferisce essenzialmente ad un fatto storico, cioè a quella corrente di pensiero che ha avuto inizio con la ripresa dell'aristotelisimo ad opera di Tommaso e si è snodata lungo tutto il resto del medioevo, l'età moderna e l'età contemporanea, sino a costituire ancora oggi una della pozioni più caratteristica e vitali del dibattito filosofico."—"L'analogia dell'essere nella tradizione . . ." (p. 13).

20. Berti provides a convenient summary of where scholars who accept the Cajetanian reading of Thomistic analogy have come out on the question of the relation between Aristotle and Thomas. Among those who admit the presence in Aristotle of the analogy of attribution, Berti numbers Franz Brentano, *Von der manigfachen Bedeutung des Seienden nach Aristoteles* (Freiburg, 1862); M.-D. Philippe, "Analogon and Analogia in the Philosophy of Aristotle," *The Thomist* 33, 1 (January, 1969), pp. 1–74; D. Dubarle, "La doctrine aristotélicienne de l'analogie et sa normalisation rationelle," *Revue des sciences philosophiques et théologiques* 53 (1969), pp. 3–40 and 212–232; P. Grenet, "Saint Thomas d'Aquin a-t-il trouvé dans Aristote 'l'*analogia entis*'?" *L'attualità della problematica aristotelica* (Padua, 1970), pp. 153–175. Berti notes that scholars of a Thomist persuasion have been prone to this view. Among those who reject it—allowing that what is called analogy of attribution, though not called that by Aristotle, has its roots in his work, but denying that anything like an analogy of being can be found there—are F. A. Trendelenburg, *Geschichte der Kategorienlehre* (Berlin, 1846), pp. 152–157; G. L. Muskin, *De vocis analogiae significatione ac usu apud Aristotelem* (Groningen, 1943); J. Hirschberger, "Paronymie und Analogie bei Aristoteles," *Philosophische Jahrbuch* 68 (1960), pp. 191–203; J. Owens, "Analogy as a Thomistic Approach to Being," *Mediaeval Studies* 24 (1962), pp. 303–322; A. De Muralt, "Comment dire l'être? Le problème de l'être et de ses significations chez Aristote," *Studia Philosophica* 23 (1963), pp. 109–162; P. Aubenque, "Les origines de la doctrine de l'analogie de l'être," *Les études philosophiques* 103 (1978), pp. 3–12.

which he is commenting. What we find in the text is rather discussions of things said in many ways but with reference to one among them, *pros hen* equivocals. Our contention is that what Aristotle means by such controlled equivocation, and the accounts he gives of it, are exactly what Thomas means when he speaks of analogous names.

What then of passages in which Aristotle *does* speak of analogy? We have seen above that a selection of such passages and Thomas's comments on them show how unhelpful, indeed misleading, it is to try to force these Aristotelian passages into the procrustean bed of the Cajetanian division. *Aristotle never uses the Greek term to speak of what Thomas calls analogous names.* Aristotle's use of the Greek, consequently, is not to be understood as referring to a kind of analogous name. The passage Cajetan misreads alerts us to Thomas's awareness that sometimes ἀναλογία does not refer to the order among several meanings of the same name but to an order and inequality in things. Indeed, the primary meaning of ἀναλογία in Aristotle involves real relations. The upshot is that, for Thomas, 'analogy' itself is an analogous name, having a plurality of meanings, and the controlling one is not that of an orderly inequality of the meanings of a common name. The primary meaning of ἀναλογία is found in mathematics, namely, the relation or proportion between quantities, numerical (discrete) or geometrical (continuous). The term then comes to mean relations outside the category of quantity. And, finally, it comes to be used—by Thomas, though he does not regard himself as the originator of this meaning—of those names Aristotle called πρὸς ἕν equivocals. That is my argument.

If Cajetan had not confused the analogy of names and the analogy of 'analogy' (according to one of whose meanings some names are called analogous), he would have been closer to the mark, and he would have seen that Latin usage is simply more expansive than is the Greek. The attempt to make Greek usage regulative of Latin necessarily led to the contention that, since there are Latin meanings of ἀναλογία with no counterpart in Greek usage, Latin involves an abuse of the word. Indeed, some of the things Latins call analogy are not really analogy. What is really analogy is what Aristotle used the Greek term to talk about, a similarity of proportions, a proportionality.[21] But neither in Aristotle nor in Thomas is *proportionality* equivalent to *analogous naming*.

To make this point, I examined passages in Thomas's commentaries on Aristotle which show (a) the correlation between *multipliciter dictitur* in Aristotle and *analogice dicitur* in Thomas, and also show (b) that, when Aristotle speaks of analogy, Thomas as commentator does not understand him to be speaking of analogous naming.[22]

What Has Been Accomplished?

Now that this argument is successfully completed, it will be asked what has been accomplished. If the Greek term is never used by Aristotle to mean analogous naming, but the Latins use the loan word to mean all the things Aristotle meant by it *and* analogous naming, so what? One answer is that getting clear on this will free us from misinterpretations of Aristotle, and surely that is not nothing. The conclusion of this chapter, coupled with that of the first, should dissuade us from asking the questions enumerated above about analogy of attribution and analogy of proportionality in Aristotle, and that too is not nothing. But the significance of my two arguments goes far deeper. If Aristotle confines his use of *analogia* to real relations, to relations among things as they exist, and if analogous naming is explained on the level of things as they are known, and if paying attention to this distinction is what separates Aristotle from Plato who, Thomas frequently says, confused the *modi essendi* and the *modi praedicandi*—if all that, then our clarifications preserve the distinction between logical accounts and accounts of things as they are.

21. I am not suggesting that Cajetan consciously opted for real relations among things and rejected relations among the several meanings of a single name. Rather, he makes an amalgam of the real (*secundum esse*) and the logical (*secundum intentionem*) to fashion 'real' analogy, the analogy of proper proportionality, a monster that would have been rejected both by Aristotle and by Thomas.

22. M.-D. Philippe, *art. cit.*, pp. 41–44, although he is writing about analogy in Aristotle, devotes himself in these pages on First Philosophy to the discussion of πολλαχῶς λεγόμενα. His conclusion is significant. "There is, then, a certain *order* among these diverse meanings of being. If there is an order, there are relations. But then, are not these terms which are said in various ways said according to analogy? Aristotle does not explicitly say this" (p. 44).

PART TWO

ANALOGOUS NAMES

THE PROSPECT BEFORE US

There is no extended formal discussion of analogy in the writings of St. Thomas Aquinas. What we find are many identifications of terms as analogous and, here and there, the elements of a formal account of what it is such names are instances of. Aquinas's teaching on analogy, accordingly, must be gleaned from a variety of places in his work and fashioned into a systematic account. One who develops such an account and calls it Thomistic must therefore mean that (a) the elements of the doctrine are drawn from Thomas, and (b) the systematic statement of doctrine is suggested by and/or compatible with what Thomas explicitly says. Thus it is that Cajetan and many others in his wake have sought to formulate the account Thomas did not write. This book is an effort in that same line, with the commendable difference that it is preferable to all the others.

In Part One we called into question the value of Cajetan's *De nominum analogia* as a guide to what Thomas explicitly and implicitly says about analogous names, and we gave reasons to question Cajetan's understanding of the relation between Aristotle and Thomas on these matters.

Cajetan's misunderstanding of a text in Thomas's commentary

on the *Sentences* of Peter Lombard, which he wrongly took to be a list of types of analogous names, continues to influence even those who set out to criticize Cajetan. The Cajetanian interpretation has flowed over into Aristotelian studies, and we find eminent scholars wondering whether Thomas's 'analogy of being' is to be found in Aristotle.[1] No doubt is expressed that it is to be found in St. Thomas. And no wonder. Cardinal Cajetan maintained that the only kind of analogous name that was truly an analogous name was the misbegotten hybrid he called proper proportionality whose principal role was played in metaphysics.

The thesis of Part One was that there is no basis in St. Thomas for the Cajetanian division of analogous names. This thesis has the consequence of making the contrast between names analogous by attribution and names analogous by proper proportionality without value for interpreting St. Thomas. Nonetheless, both friend and foe of Cajetan continue to use this terminology. *It is not simply that it cannot be found in Aristotle; it cannot be found in St. Thomas.*

In Part One , however, we did not argue that *what* Thomas means by analogous names is different from, in conflict with, or even an advance on, what Aristotle means by "things said in many ways but with reference to some one nature." The two men teach the same thing about the behavior of such words but they dub their doctrines differently.

In Part Two we put before the reader a systematic account of what Thomas Aquinas means by analogous names. This part also has a negative thesis, and it is this: Just as Aristotle never used the Greek term ἀναλογία to refer to what Thomas Aquinas calls analogous names, so Thomas Aquinas never used the Latin term ἀναλογία to refer to what has come to be called the analogy of being.

1. It is of passing interest to note that when Pierre Aubenque pursues this question he writes as follows: "Si la doctrine de l'analogie de l'être a occupé une place importante dans l'histoire de la métaphysique, ce ne fut pas chez Aristote, mais au Moyen Age, en particulier chez Thomas d'Aquin. La formulation et la justification la plus claire de cette doctrine sous sa forme thomiste se recontrent aux chapitres 4 et 5 du petit traité de jeunesse *De ente et essentia,* même si le terme *analogia* ne s'y trouve pas employé" ("Sur la naissance de la doctrine pseudo-aristotlicienne de l'analogie de l'être," *Les Etudes philosophiques,* no. 3–4 [1989], p. 292). "Even though," as he says, "the term 'analogy' is not used!"

THREE

HOW WORDS SIGNIFY

When a term is said to be analogous, it is contrasted with univocal and purely equivocal terms. That is, the analogous term is a type of shared or common term. Things are said to be named univocally when the term they share receives exactly the same account as applied to each, whereas things are said to be named equivocally when, though they share the same term—the same orthographic symbol or the same vocal sound—the term receives quite unrelated accounts as applied to them. The analogous term is located between these two.

It might be thought that it would be better to say that these are different ways in which words or terms can be used. A case could perhaps be made for this, but not as an accurate portrayal of Thomas's teaching. Besides, we will find that the distinction between meaning and use provides a way of distinguishing analogous from metaphorical terms.

There are things presupposed to understanding even this preliminary account of analogous names. What is a name? What is it for a name to signify? And, most broadly, what kinds of questions are these?

Like his mentor Aristotle, Thomas takes seriously the distinction between types of inquiry and, for example, dwells on the formal difference between an argument in natural philosophy and one in mathematics. To what discipline or science do the questions we have just formulated fall?

In the *Summa theologiae*, asking whether God can be named, Thomas begins the discussion by invoking what Aristotle had to say in *On Interpretation*.

Respondeo dicendum quod, secundum Philosophum, voces sunt signa intellectuum, et intellectus sunt rerum similitudines. Et sic patet quod voces referuntur ad res significandas, mediante conceptione intellectus. Secundum igitur quod aliquid a nobis intellectu cognosci potest, sic a nobis potest nominari. (*ST,* Ia, q. 13, a.1)

I answer that it should be said that according to Aristotle voiced sounds are signs of what is understood and concepts are similitudes of the things understood. Thus it is clear that words are referred to the things to be signified by way of the conception of intellect. Insofar then as something can be known by our intellect, it can be named by us.

This triadic account of signification—vocal sound, mental grasp, thing—is the great presupposition of the distinction between univocal, equivocal, and analogous names. The reference is to a work numbered among the logical books of Aristotle. Presumably what is taught in a book of logic is logic and therefore this account of the signification of names is a logical doctrine. What does that mean? How does Thomas formally characterize logic?

One of the ways in which Thomas arrays the various disciplines is according to their pedagogical order, the most effective way of acquiring them, the *ordo addiscendi*. He sets this forth as Aristotelian, but it is Aristotelian in the way in which this book conveys the Thomistic doctrine of analogy. Thomas puts together a number of passages in Aristotle and the result is the following:

Primo quidem incipientes a logica quae modum scientiarum tradit, secundo procedentes ad mathematicam cuius etiam pueri possunt esse capaces, tertio ad naturalem philosophiam quae propter experientiam tempore indiget, quarto autem ad moralem philosophiam cuius iuvenis esse conveniens auditor non potest, ultimo autem scientiae divinae insistebant quae considerat primas entium causas. (*In librum de causis,* proemium)

Beginning with logic which deals with the mode of the sciences, second, going on to mathematics of which even boys are capable, third, to natural philosophy which, because of the experience required needs time, fourth, to moral philosophy of which youth are not appropriate students, finally they pursued divine science which considers the first causes of beings.

Logic teaches the *modus scientiarum.* Thomas commented on two of Aristotle's logical works, *On Interpretation,* which is unfinished, and the *Posterior Analytics.* His prefaces, or proemia, to these commentaries are of help in grasping what Thomas took logic to be and how he saw these books deal with parts of logic. The proemium to the commentary on the book Thomas called *De interpretatione* begins by recalling a distinction between two kinds of mental act, *operationes intellectus.* The first kind, called the understanding of indivisibles, is that through which the intellect grasps the essences of things; the second is that whereby the intellect composes and divides. This distinction is already found in the *Categories.*[1] Reasoning is a third operation *secundum quod ratio procedit a notis ad inquisitionem ignotorum.* An argument can be analyzed into its constituent propositions, and they in turn can be analyzed into their indivisible constituents. "The first of these operations is ordered to the second, because there can only be composition and division of apprehended simple things. The second is ordered to the third, since it is from some known truth, to which the intellect gives its assent, that we proceed to accept with certainty some unknown things."[2]

Thomas, when he introduces this distinction between two kinds

---

1. Found, that is, in terms of the linguistic expression of the mental acts. "Of things that are said, some involve combination while others are said without combination. Examples of those involving combination are: man runs, man wins; and of those without combination: man, ox, runs, wins" (1a17–19).

2. *Proemium,* n. 2 = p. 5, ll. 8–14. The Leonine Commission has issued a second revised edition of the commentary on the *De interpretatione. Opera Omnia* Tomus I* 1, *Expositio Libri Peryermenias* (Rome, 1989); the first edition divided the texts into *lectiones* and numbered the paragraphs, a format which was reproduced in the Marietti edition, S. Thomae Aquinatis, *In Aristotelis Libros Peri Hermeneias et Posteriorum Analyticorum Expositio* (Turin: Marietti Editori Ltd., 1955). My citations will provide a concordance of the two editions. For nearly a century references were made to lessons and paragraph number, and indeed to the first edition; by dropping this editorial convenience, the editors of the Leonine create a chasm between the newly edited text and the history of interpretation of the work.

of mental acts, refers to Aristotle's *On the Soul*, a work he takes to be part of natural philosophy, more specifically psychology, and it seems right so to characterize talk about mental acts, rational activity. Thomas calls logic a rational science, *scientia rationalis*, which considers what pertains to those three operations of mind. Is logic psychology, and, if not, how do the two disciplines differ?

What is Logic?

By saying that logic treats the mode of knowledge (*modus scientiarum*), Thomas indicates that logic deals with something that is piggybacked upon knowledge. In the proemium to the commentary on the *Posterior Analytics*, he speaks of logic as an art. Art distinguishes human activities from those of brutes since the latter are unlearned and fixed: whatever variation we may notice in the way grey squirrels build nests, gather and bury food, and dig it up again, the variations are severely bound by the instinctive. Or, as Aristotle puts it, animals other than man are provided by nature with clothing and protection against the elements, whereas man has been given the prehensile hand, the instrument of instruments, and reason, whose instrument the hand is, and then has been left to fashion for himself what he will wear, what his home will be, what foods he will eat, and how they will be prepared, etc. It is not, of course, that human beings decide that they will take nourishment; that is a natural necessity. What is contingent is what we will take as nourishment, and the cultivation and preparation of it. The arts of hunting, fishing, farming, and cooking presuppose nature, but man's nature is inchoative and must be perfected by putting one's mind to achieving the naturally given end.[3]

If any art is a way of acting modified by taking thought, that is, if every art is rational, logic is doubly rational, since it is the very activity of reasoning that it directs. We cannot not think, but we

---

3. "Et inde est quod ad actus humanos faciliter et ordinate perficiendos diversae artes deserviunt. Nihil enim aliud ars esse videtur, quam certa ordinatio rationis quomodo per determinata media ad debitum finem actus humani perveniant" (*In Post. Analytic.*, proemium, n. 1 = I, 1, ll. 7–12). The definition of art is taken from *Nicomachean Ethics*, VI, 4, 1140a6–10.

can think well or badly, and logic is the art of thinking well. Not only is it an art, it is the art of arts.[4]

Logic is an ordering, and it deals with the logical order. What is the logical order?

Uno modo secundum quod iste ordo est adinventus per intellectum et attributus ei quod relative dicitur; et huiusmodi sunt relationes quae attribuentur ab intellectu rebus intellectis, prout sunt intellectae, sicut relatio generis et speciei: has enim relationes ratio adinvenit considerando ordinem eius quod est in intellectu ad res quae sunt extra, vel etiam ordinem intellectuum ad invicem. (*Q. D. de pot.*, q. 7, a. 11)

In one way insofar as the order is established by reason and attributed to what is said relatively; these are the relations attributed by intellect to things understood, as they are understood, like the relation of genus and species. Reason establishes these relations in considering the order of that which is in the intellect to the things outside it, or, too, the order of concepts to one another.

This passage illustrates what is meant by the logical order, and what it means for reason to order its own activity by the formation of the genus and species. Since genera and species are types of universal, the so-called problem of universals provides an apt way of grasping what Thomas means by logic and by the subject matter of logic. Elsewhere he illustrates the logical order in a way that links up with our present concern. "There is another order which reason, by considering, introduces into its own act, for example, when it orders its concepts to one another, *and the signs of concepts, which are significant voiced sounds*."[5]

Universals

Perhaps the most succinct statement Thomas ever gave of the status of such logical relations as genus and species is found in the *De*

---

4. "Quae non solum rationalis est ex hoc, quod est secundum rationem (quod est omnibus artibus commune); sed etiam ex hoc, quod est circa ipsum actum rationis sicut circa propriam materiam. Et ideo videtur esse ars artium, quia in actu rationis nos dirigit, a quo omnes artes procedunt" (*ibid.*, nn. 2–3 = I, 1, ll. 25–31).Thus Thomas here provides the ground for the starting point of the proemium of the commentary on the *De interpretatione*. He goes on: "Oportet igitur logicae partes accipere secundum diversitatem actuum rationis" (n. 3 = ll. 32–33).

5. "Alius autem est ordo, quem ratio considerando facit in proprio actu, puta cum ordinat conceptus suos adinvicem, et signa conceptuum, quia sunt voces significativae" (*In I Ethic.*, lect. 1, n. 1; cf. *ST*, Ia, q. 3, a. 4, ad 2).

ente et essentia. Genera and species are kinds of universal, a universal being that which is said of many. Porphyry, in his *Isagoge,* written to facilitate understanding of the *Categories,* provided the definitions that became canonical in the Middle Ages. A genus is something that is said of many specifically different subjects. A species is something that is said of numerically different subjects. The *Categories* itself introduces a distinction between first or primary and second or secondary particular substances.

A *substance*—that which is called a substance most strictly, primarily, and most of all—is that which is said neither of a subject nor in a subject, e.g. the individual man or the individual horse. The species in which the things primarily called substances are, are called *secondary substances,* as also are the genera of these species. For example, the individual man belongs in a species, man, and animal is the genus of the species; so these—both man and animal—are called secondary substances. (2a11–19)

In Book Seven of the *Metaphysics,* at the beginning of his study of substance, Aristotle notes that four things are called substance: the universal, the genus, the essence, and the subject. How does this division relate to the division in the *Categories?* Genus and universal can be linked, and they match secondary substance, while subject matches primary substance, What about essence? It is omitted in the *Categories,* Thomas suggests, because it does not fall within the order of the categories except as a principle. "For it is not a genus or a species or an individual but the formal principle of them all."[6]

In the *De ente et essentia,* Thomas is concerned with the differences between the following statements:

1. Man is rational.
2. Man is seated.
3. Man is a species.

6. "Unde patet quod fere eadem est divisio substantiae hic posita, cum illa quae ponitur in *Praedicamentis.* Nam per subiectum intelligitur hic substantia prima. Quod autem dixit genus et universale, quod videtur ad genus et species pertinere, continetur sub substantiis secundis. Hoc autem quod quid erat esse hic ponitur, sed ibi praetermittitur, quia non cadit in praedicamentorum ordine nisi sicut principium. Neque enim est genus neque species neque individuum sed horum omniumn formale principium" (*In VII Metaphysic.,* lect. 2, n. 1275).

All three statements are true. Their differences can be brought out by conjoining each of them with another truth:

4. Socrates is a man.

The conjunction of (1) and (4) yields, "Socrates is rational," but from the conjunction of (2) and (4) we would hesitate to conclude that Socrates is seated. Of course, if (2) is true, it is so in virtue of Socrates or someone else being seated, but this conjunction is not necessary. Someone can be a human being and for all that not be seated. If someone is a human being *and* is seated, it just happens to be true, but it does not just happen to be true that a human being is rational. To be rational is part and parcel of being human.

This distinction between what belongs *per se* or as such to a nature and what just happens to belong to it, the *per accidens,* is asymmetrical. Whatever has human nature will have that which is part and parcel of it, whereas what is said of the nature because some instance of that nature happens to have or be it, is not said of it *per se*. What pertains to the nature *per se* will necessarily be true of the individual having that nature, but what is true of the individual is not necessarily true of the nature. This is why the conjunction of (2) and (4) does not yield, "Socrates is seated." Of course it may be true that Socrates is seated, but it is not true of him simply because he is human.

What now of the conjunction of (3) and (4)? Although Socrates is a man and man is a species, we would not conclude that Socrates is a species. To be a species is to be something predicable of numerically different things. If to be a species is truly predicable of man, it does not pertain to human nature *per se*. Nor is it accidentally true of the nature because it is true of some individual having that nature. To be a species is not true of any material individual. If species is truly predicated of man, and if it does not pertain to human nature *per se,* and if *per se* and *per accidens* exhaust the possibilities, then species just happens to be true of human nature. In virtue of what?

Relinquitur ergo quod ratio speciei accidat naturae humanae secundum illud esse quod habet in intellectu. Ipsa enim natura humana habet esse in intellectu abstractum ab omnibus individuantibus, et ideo habet rationem uniformem ad omnia individua quae sunt extra animam, prout aequaliter est similitudo omnium et inducens in cognitionem omnium, inquantum sunt homines. Et ex hoc quod talem relationem habet ad omnia individua, intellectus adinvenit rationem speciei et attribuit sibi. (*De ente et essentia*, ed. Baur, p. 33, l.17–p. 34, l.8)

What remains, therefore, is that the notion of species befalls human nature according to the existence it has in the mind. Human nature exists in the mind abstracted from all individuating traits, and thus it has a notion uniform to all the individuals that are outside the soul insofar as it is equally the likeness of them all and leads to knowledge of them all to the extent that they are men. From the fact that it has such a relation to all individuals, the mind fashions the notion of species that it attributes to it.

The universal is a logical relation that attaches to the nature as known. The nature, grasped by the intellect in abstraction from what is true of it in this individual or that, is related by the mind to those individuals. As known the nature is abstract, immaterial, universal—none of these traits characterize the nature as such; they are accidental to it. "For humanity is something in a thing, but it does not have there the note of universal, since there is not some humanity common to many outside the mind, but insofar as it is grasped by the intellect, there is conjoined to it by the operation of the intellect an intention thanks to which it is called a species."[7]

If only individuals exist *in rerum natura*, it would appear that the human mind, in understanding them universally, abstractly, immaterially, understands them otherwise than as they are. To know things as they are thus becomes logically impossible. Thomas suggests a distinction that permits us to avoid this vertiginous conclusion. To understand a thing otherwise than as it is seems to be a good definition of false understanding. But understanding something otherwise than as it is can be taken in several ways. To understand that a singular thing is universal, or a concrete thing is abstract, or a material thing is immaterial, would indeed be a false understanding. To understand a singular thing universally, a concrete thing abstractly, a material thing immaterially, modifies our understanding, not the thing understood.[8]

7. "Humanitas enim est aliquid in re, non tamen ibi habet rationem universalis, cum non sit extra animam aliqua humanitas multis communis; sed secundum quod accipitur in intellectu, adjungitur ei per operationem intellectus intentio secundum quam dicitur species" (*I Sent.*, d. 19, q. 5, a. 1).
8. Cum ergo dicitur quod intellectus est falsus qui intelligit rem aliter quam sit,

The relations of reason with which the logician is concerned are called *secunda intellecta* or second intentions.[9] The natures the mind knows are likenesses of things outside the mind and thus means of knowing them; these are first intentions. Second intentions are the relations that attach to the nature as known; it is by reflecting on its own activities that the mind becomes aware of these logical relations.[10] First we know the things that are; secondly we know the way we know them. "Second" thus has a chronological import as well as a second-order connotation.

The Signification of Words

Thomas illustrates what he means by the logical order by referring to the nature of universal; but, as we have seen, he also assigns the signification of words to the logical order. "There is another order that reason, by considering, introduces into its own act, for example, when it orders its concepts to one another, *and the signs of concepts, which are significant voiced sounds.*"[11]

Several disciplines are concerned with language. The philosophy of nature considers vocal sounds as effects that a certain kind of animate being produces, namely those with respiratory systems.[12] The philosopher of nature defines *vox* as follows: "vox sit respirati percussio aeris ad arteriam vocalem, quae quidem percussio fit ab

---

verum est si ly aliter referatur ad rem intellectam. Tunc enim intellectus est falsus quando intelligit rem esse aliter quam sit (. . .) Non est autem verum quod proponitur si ly aliter accipiatur ex parte intelligentis. Est enim absque falsitate ut alius sit modus intelligentis in intelligendo, quam modus rei in essendo; quia intellectum est in intelligente immaterialiter per modum intellectus, non autem materialiter per modum rei materialis (*ST,* Ia, q. 85, a. 1 ad 1). See also *ST,* Ia, q. 13, a. 12, ad 3.

9. Cf. *I Sent.,* d. 23, q. 1, a. 3.

10. Prima enim intellecta sunt res extra animam, in quae primo intellectus intelligenda fertur. Secunda autem intellecta dicuntur intentiones consequentes modum intelligendi: hoc enim secundo intellectus intelligit in quantum reflectitur supra se ipsum, intelligens se intelligere et modum quo intelligit. Secundum ergo hanc positionem sequeretur quod relatio (between God and creature) non sit in rebus extra animam, sed in solo intellectu, sicut intentio generis et speciei, et secundarum substantiarum" (*Q. D. de pot.,* q. 7, a.9).

11. "Alius autem est ordo, quem ratio considerando facit in proprio actu, puta cum ordinat conceptus suos ad invicem, et signa conceptuum, quia sunt voces significativae" (*In I Ethic.,* lect. 1, n. 1; cf. *ST,* Ia, q. 3, a. 4 ad 2).

12. *On the Soul,* II, 8.

anima, quae est in his partibus, idest principaliter in corde."[13] Not
a very interesting definition for our purposes, perhaps, but it expresses what is physical in the word. It does not, however, enable us
to distinguish the cries of animals from human conversation.

The word is discussed in grammar as well, and it will be useful
to ask Thomas what the difference between the grammarian's and
the logician's treatment of language is. Unfortunately, his remarks
on the distinction are largely *obiter dicta*. Grammar is said to be
the *scientia recte loquendi*,[14] its concern is the *congrua vocum con-
structio*,[15] and, since any science studies opposites, it deals with in-
congruous constructions as well.[16] Though the grammarian, like the
logician, is concerned with words taken alone and in composition
with other words, his is, so to say, a more artificial concern than
the logician's. Logical relations are founded on concepts, and the
nature of these concepts dictates the nature of logical relations;
grammar, on the other hand, deals with the purely conventional, and
if it is called a science, 'science' must be taken in the broadest
sense.[17] Logic is ordered to knowledge of real things, and this makes
the written word of little interest to it, whereas grammar is necessarily concerned with the written language.[18] Indeed, St. Thomas
will oppose logic and the philosophy of nature to grammar, saying
that the former are concerned with the nature of things, while grammar is concerned with the *modus significandi*.[19] Grammar, as pure
art, defines in an artistic way; thus the substantive is such because

13. *In II de anima*, lect. 18, n. 476 [= Leonine, cap. xviii, lines 130–144].
14. *Q. D. de ver.*, q. 24, a. 6.
15. *In I Periherm.* lect. 7, n. 6.
16. *In IV Metaphysic.*, lect. 3, 564.
17. See Sheilah O'Flynn [Brennan], "The First Meaning of 'Rational Process'
According to the *Expositio in Boethium De trinitate*," *Laval théologique et philosophique* 10 (1954), pp. 167–188.
18. *In I Periherm.*, lect. 2, n. 3. The difference may be illustrated by noting that,
whereas the spoken and written words that signify logical relations are conventional
or arbitrary, these relations themselves are not, since they have their foundation in
natures as known. The foundation of logical relations introduces the note of necessity thanks to which logic is science in the strict sense, and not merely an art, as
grammar is.
19. See *In II Sent.*, d. 35, q. 1, a. 2 ad 5: ". . . dicendum quod passio potest
sumi dupliciter: vel quantum ad naturam rei prout logicus et naturalis passionem
considerat, et hoc modo non oportet omnem poenam passionem esse, sed quandam
poenam, scilicet poenam sensus: vel quantum ad modum significandi, prout gram-
maticus considerat . . ."

it imitates substance, signifying *per modum substantiae,* in the manner of substance.[20] Needless to say, a substantive such as "whiteness" is in reality an accident. The grammarian's use of the terms "substance" and "quality" does not correspond to the categories of the same names that are distinguished by the logician.[21] The conclusion is not that grammar is unimportant. In the order of learning proposed by St. Thomas, the trivium of the liberal arts— grammar, rhetoric, logic—was presupposed to any further study, and grammar preceded logic.[22] The disciplines concerned with the word, the *artes sermocinales,* had a priority because they dealt with what is most obvious to us or most necessary for learning other things. Not that concern with language ends with the trivium. The wise man, the metaphysician as well as the theologian, will exhibit concern with words and signification.[23] But let us return to the logician's concern with language and meaning.

When Thomas speaks of the way words signify, the doctrine presupposed to the distinction of some shared terms into univocal, equivocal, or analogous terms, he employs a triadic account that he explicitly identifies as Aristotelian. Thomas bases his teaching on the way words signify on the following text of Aristotle:

Spoken words are the symbols of mental experience, and written words are symbols of spoken words. Just as all men have not the same writing, so all men have not the same speech sounds, but the mental experiences, which these [speech sounds] directly symbolize, are the same for all, as also are those things of which our experiences are the images. This matter has, however, been discussed in my treatise about the soul, for it belongs to an investigation distinct from that which lies before us. (*On Interpretation,* 16a3–8)

There are four elements in play: things, concepts, verbal expression, and script. These elements enable Aristotle to state this proportionality or analogy.

20. *In V Metaphysic.,* lect. 9, n. 894.
21. *In I Sent.,* d. 22, q. 1, a. 1 ad 3.
22. *In Boethii de trinitate,* q. 5, a. 1 ad 3.
23. To the objection that the science concerned with *res* will not be concerned with *nomina,* St Thomas replies, "sed dicendum quod (. . .) theologia, inquantum est principalis omnium scientiarum, aliquid se habet de omnibus scientiis; et ideo non solum res, sed nominum significationes pertracta: quia ad salutem consequendam non solum est necessaria fides de veritate rerum, sed etiam vocalis confessio per nomina" (*In I Sent.,* d. 22, *expositio textus* [ed. Mandonnet], I, p. 543). For the metaphysician's interest in words, see *In V Metaphysic.,* lect. 1, n. 749.

$$Speech \quad : \quad Script$$
$$Concepts \quad : \quad Speech$$

The relation between the elements of each proportion is expressed in the same way: speech and script are *symbols* of concepts and speech respectively. Not only are these two proportions similar, but we can also extend the analogy and add a third.

$$Script \quad : \quad Speech \quad : \quad Concepts$$
$$Speech \quad : \quad Concepts \quad : \quad Things$$

At the outset, Aristotle uses *symbola* to describe what spoken words are relative to concepts AND what script is relative to speech. But, after noticing that written and spoken language differ from people to people and from place to place, he uses the word *semeia* for the relation between speech and concepts, because the latter are the same for all despite differences of spoken and written language. Why? Because concepts are the images or likenesses of things.

An Unsympathetic Reading

Many people nowadays encounter this text of *On Interpretation* in an edition whose commentary is scarcely calculated to commend the Aristotelian passage to them. It may be well, accordingly, to clear away this obstacle to a sympathetic reading.

Ackrill says that "the present passage is intended as an argument for the view that language is conventional."[24] What is the argument he discerns?

Different people (or peoples) confront the same things and situations, and have the same impressions of them and thoughts about them (likeness is a natural relation); but they use different spoken or written words to express their thoughts (words are conventional symbols).[25]

Ackrill formulates this argument, not to defend or commend it, but to criticize it. It is his assumption that Aristotle is seeking to establish the conventional character of language, and to this he poses two objections.

24. *Aristotle's Categories and De Interpretatione*, translated with notes by J. L. Ackrill (Oxford: Clarendon Press, 1963), p. 113.
25. Ibid.

Objection 1: "Of course it is not true that all men meet the same things or have the same thoughts."[26]

Objection 2: "Nor would the mere fact that different words are equally capable of expressing a given thought be enough to prove that the words are significant only by convention, not by nature. (The choice of material for an axe is *not* a matter of convention; the nature of an axe's task imposes limits. Yet there may be a variety of materials any of which would do— though not every material would do. Thus the possibility of people's using differently made tools for the same job does not show that it is purely a matter of convention how a tool for a job is made.) Aristotle would have made his point more cogently if he had said that different men *may* share the same thought though expressing it in different words, and that there is *no* restriction on what sounds or written marks could be used by people as words to express their thoughts. The whole question whether language is conventional or natural is brilliantly discussed in Plato's *Cratylus*."[27]

Ad primum. The question is rather what happens when men meet the same things. Surely Ackrill does not wish to attribute to Aristotle the claim that each and every man has identically the same experience, the same adventures, the same environment, as if Aristotle did not realize that little Athenians have different things before their eyes than little Spartans. Aristotle's assumption is that human beings can and do sometimes confront the same things. Does Ackrill wish to contest that they would have the same thoughts about those things? In order to contend that they have different thoughts, Ackrill must have a criterion by which to determine that they have the same thoughts. Perhaps he means that they do not have numerically the same concepts. That surely is true, but are their numerically different thoughts of the same things? If not, he can scarcely make his objection, so that in making it he shows it is not *ad rem*.

Ad secundum. The fact that in making an artifact, which is the artifact it is because of the task it has, men have the choice of a finite range of materials suggests that there is no natural need to select one kind of material rather than another. Ackrill objects to describing this as conventional, but then one would have to ask what *he* means by 'conventional' and our interest is Aristotle rather than

---

26. Ibid.
27. Ibid., p. 114.

Ackrill. Of course, Aristotle does not use the term 'conventional', What he says is that speech and script vary, just as one might say that there are stone axes, bronze axes, and iron axes. The material is not the same. In his effort to assist Aristotle, Ackrill apparently thinks that saying that there is *no* restriction on what sounds or marks might be used is the way to show that language is conventional. But, of course, he has already restricted the material to sounds and marks.

Ackrill is simply wrong to see the point of this passage to be an argument for the conventional character of language. Since Aristotle *assumes* that speech and script differ, he can hardly be embarked on proving this. A small mistake in the beginning snowballs as a discussion progresses, as Aristotle effectively said elsewhere. What Aristotle does do here is contrast the differences that show up in speech and script with the way in which concepts relate to things as their likenesses. Since Ackrill has, in his opening remarks, dismissed the notion of likeness or similarity, he is not in a position to understand the passage. It is because concepts are likenesses of things and naturally express them that they differ from speech and script. By trying to read the passage as an argument for the differences of spoken and written language, Ackrill fails to be of help to one seeking to understand Aristotle.

A Sympathetic Reading

Thomas Aquinas's reading of *On Interpretation* is in marked contrast to Ackrill's. Thomas is not a tutor correcting a pupil's paper, but a student approaching a master. He is attentive, receptive, on the *qui vive* for the subtleties and turns of the text. And he gets it right.

Sunt ergo ea que sunt in uoce earum que sunt in anima passionum note. —Et ea que scribuntur eorum que sunt in uoce.[28] (16a3–8)

Things that are of speech are signs of the soul's passions and what is written signs of what is spoken.

28. See John Magee, *Boethius on Mind and Signification* (Leiden: E. J. Brill, 1990), *passim*.

Thomas first places the text. Aristotle has begun by saying that he will first discuss the noun and the verb and then go on to treat negation and affirmation. That is, he will consider first incomplex significant voiced sounds and then complex significant speech susceptible of truth and falsity.[29] Before turning to the discussion of noun and then verb, Aristotle sets down things common to both complex and incomplex significant speech.

The text begins by mentioning three things that suggest a fourth: speech (τὰ ἐν τῇ φωνῇ), concept (τὰ ἐν τῇ ψυχῇ παθήματα), and script (τὰ γραφόμενα)—these point to the things that are.[30] Ackrill translates as 'mental experiences' the phrase τὰ παθήματα τῆς ψυχῆς. The Latin renders it *passiones animae*. Spoken language, communication with others, presupposes others, of course, suggesting the political or social basis of language. A solitary man would have no need to speak, except perhaps to imaginary interlocutors or for the same reason one hums, but it is the positive, nonhypothetical side that Thomas stresses. It is because man is naturally political and social that speech is necessary, and that is also why those without a common language live together only with difficulty. Logic is less interested in script than in speech.[31]

Why does Aristotle use this phrase: vocal sounds are symbols of *passions of the soul*. The phrase, Thomas notes,[32] suggests emo-

---

29. The 'therefore' (*ergo, οὖν*) is taken by Thomas to mean that, since we will talk about noun and verb, we must first talk about what they have in common, namely being signficant speech. The mention of talk, thought, and writing, Thomas takes to follow quite naturally: *dixerat enim dicendum esse de nomine et verbo et aliis huiusmodi; hec autem tripliciter habent esse: uno quidem in conceptione intellectus; alio modo in prolatione uocis; tercio modo in descriptione litterarum* (ll. 67–72).

30. "Est ergo considerandum quod circa primum tria proponit, ex quorum uno intelligitur quartum: proponit enim scripturam, uoces et animae passiones, ex quibus intelliguntur res: nam passio est ex impressione alicuius agentis, et sic passiones anime originem habent ab ipsis rebus" (I. 2, 20–25).

31. "Set, quia logica ordinatur ad cognitionem de rebus sumendam, significatio uocum, que est inmediata ipsis conceptionibus intellectus, pertinet ad principalem considerationem ipsius, significatio autem litterarum, tanquam magis remota, non pertinet ad eius considerationem, set magis ad considerationem gramatici; et ideo, exponens ordinem significationum, non incipit a litteris, set a uocibus" (ibid., 49–56).

32. Ibid., 88–95. A little later, Thomas notes that this use of 'passions of the soul' to signify ideas led some to doubt that this was an authentic Aristotelian work, because such usage is not customary with him. On the contrary, in *On the Soul* he

tions, feelings, and passions like anger and joy, which are naturally signified by groans and cries and the like. If Aristotle meant sounds like these, the text would make no sense. The discussion is about sounds whose significance is due to human convention; consequently, 'passions of the soul' should be taken to mean mind's ideas. These ideas are immediately signified by nouns and verbs and speech, Aristotle maintains.[33] Why?

Non enim potest esse quod significent inmediate ipsas res, ut ex ipso modo significandi apparet: significat enim hoc nomen *homo* naturam humanam in abstractione a singularibus. Unde non potest esse quod significet immediate hominem singularem. Vnde Platonici posuerunt quod significaret ipsam ydeam hominis separatam; set, quia hec secundum suam abstractionem non subsistit realiter secundum sentenciam Aristotelis, set est in solo intellectu, ideo necesse fuit Aristoteli dicere quod uoces significant intellectus conceptiones inmediate et eis mediantibus res. (ll. 100–112)

It cannot be that they immediately signify individual things themselves, as is clear from the mode itself of signifying. 'Man' signifies human nature in abstraction from singulars, so that it cannot immediately signify the singular man. That is why Platonists said that it signified the separate idea of man himself. However, because according to Aristotle's view, these do not subsist abstractly, save in the intellect, it was necessary for Aristotle to say that voiced sounds immediately signify the mind's concepts and things by way of them.

Ackrill is not alone in taking this passage of Aristotle to mean that speech first signifies 'psychological experiences' or 'psychological facts' and, after this detour, things. Is it accurate to interpret

---

does use the phrase for mental operations in Book One (402a7–10; 403a3–28), and in Book Three he says of the understanding of the possible intellect that it is a kind of receiving: *intelligere est quoddam pati* (429b25). That is to say, the word 'to suffer' or 'to receive' becomes analogous (*extenso nomine passionis ad omnem receptionem, ipsum intelligere intellectus possibilis quoddam pati est* [ll. 122–125]). See too my *Studies in Analogy*, pp. 30–33.

Thomas will give two reasons why Aristotle might have used *passiones* in this context: (a) we are moved to speak out of love or hate or some other emotion, and (b) the conception of the intellect is in a way an impression or passion from things (ll.126–133).

33. "Set nunc est sermo de uocibus significatiuis ex institutione humana, et ideo oportet passiones anime hic intelligere intellectus conceptiones, quas nomina et verba et orationes significant [immediate], secundum sentenciam Aristotilis" (ll. 95–100). The Leonine edition omits the *immediate* one finds in the (first edition) Marietti. The adverb is present however in line 111.

Aristotle to mean that speech refers to something going on in our heads? That is, is it reflexive, referring to our knowledge of things first and only then and secondarily to things? What then of his vaunted realism? Read in this way, the Aristotelian passage looks to be a version of the modern epistemological project. Thought is the first and primary object of itself and that is why speech first signifies thoughts, psychological experiences. Thomas's remark that all operations of the soul are called passions of the soul may seem to contribute to the notion that Aristotle means to say that our words first and immediately refer to psychological activity and only secondarily and through the mediation of concepts to things.

A prima facie reason for rejecting this reading is that it would seem to deprive us of any way to distinguish between such words as 'rabbit' and 'running', on the one hand, and 'idea' and 'thinking' on the other. For our purposes, even more serious than the blurring of psychological and natural terms would be the fact that the way in which the subject of logic was described would no longer be distinctive of it. If characteristic logical terms are taken to signify things as we know them and then signification in general is described as signifying things as we known them, we have a distinction without a difference.

This analysis suggests that we should not read the passage in this way. Thomas certainly does not. We have seen that the context leads him to introduce the Platonic Ideas as arising from a confusion of the way things exist with the way in which we know them. Aristotle's rejection of the Ideas reposes on this distinction, so that we are justified in rejecting the reading of the text according to which words mean things as we know them, or our psychological experience. Aristotle provides us with an alternative understanding of common nouns.

If all things are singular and common nouns range over singulars, common nouns cannot *signify* or *mean* singulars flat out, immediately, directly. It was just because he recognized this impossibility that Plato posited a separate entity, an ideal reality, of which the common noun was, so to speak, the proper name. 'Man' can directly signify Man, though not this man or that.

Imagine Plato confronting the Aristotelian doctrine as interpreted by, say, Ackrill. 'Man' immediately signifies my psychological experience of individual men, but that psychological experience is a singular event. Furthermore, I am a contingent being, not pure thought. To pin the meaning of common terms on so fragile a basis simply relocates the problem.

It is misleading to say that 'Man' signifies my thought of man or even the thought of man, as if 'man' meant man as thought about. The triad of signification is rather: SPEECH-NATURE-THING. This is Thomas's point. A common noun signifies what Thomas in the *De ente* calls the *natura absolute considerata*. The Problem of Universals thus has to be addressed in speaking of the meaning of common words.[34]

3. The Imposition of Words

How is it that vocal signs become significant? In speaking of the imposition of words or names,[35] St. Thomas distinguishes between that from which (*id a quo*) and that which the name is imposed to signify (*id ad quod nomen imponitur ad significandum*). The name is imposed from that which is most knowable to us, since we name as we know. The sensible effects of things are first and most easily known by us, and the *id a quo* will often be that which is grasped by the senses. What is signified, however, need not be these sensible effects.

Dicendum quod in significatione nominum aliud est quandoque a quo imponitur nomen ad significandum, et aliud ad quod significandum nomen imponitur: sicut hoc nomen *lapis* imponitur ab eo quod laedit pedem; non tamen imponitur ad hoc significandum, quod significet *laedens pedem*, sed ad significandum quamdam speciem corporum; alioquin omne laedens pedem esset lapis. (*ST*, Ia, q. 13, a. 2 ad 2.)

34. ". . . voces enim non proferuntur nisi ad exprimandum interiores animae passiones." Does this not suggest that Thomas Aquinas agrees with Ackrill? The answer is found in a precision Thomas makes in the next lectio. There, distinguishing significant vocal sounds into those expressive of truth and those not, Thomas writes: "*et sicut res dicitur vera per comparationem ad suam mensuram, ita etiam et sensus vel intellectus, CUIUS MENSURA EST RES EXTRA ANIMAM.*" The concept as what is primarily signified by the word is a pure sign; it is known only on reflection, when we ask, having in mind universal terms, how words mean things.

35. *Q. D. de ver.*, q. 9, a. 4 ad 12.

Note that in the signification of a name sometimes that from which it is imposed to signify is different from what it is imposed to signify. Take the word for stone which is imposed from the fact that it bruises the foot, but it is not imposed to signify that, as if it meant 'what bruises the foot,' but to signify a certain species of body. Otherwise anything that bruises the foot would be a stone.

By saying that sometimes there is a difference between the *id a quo* and the *id ad quod*, St. Thomas suggests that it can happen that there is no difference. We can see that these can be the same wherever what is signified is so manifest that there is no need to impose the word from something more manifest. The examples St. Thomas gives of words whose *id a quo* and *id ad quod* are identical are things which are absolutely basic.

Si qua vero sunt quae secundum se sunt nota nobis, ut calor, frigus, albedo et huiusmodi, non ab aliis denominantur. Unde in talibus idem est quod nomen significat et id a quo imponitur nomen ad significandum. (*ST,* Ia, q. 13, a. 8)

If there are things which we know in themselves, like heat, cold, whiteness and the like, they are not named from something else. In such cases that from which the name is imposed and what it signifies are the same.

Such things are so knowable that there is nothing more knowable from which they could be denominated; rather, other things will be denominated from them. In speaking of the object of intellect as such, we often denominate it from what is grasped by the senses and by which we come to knowledge of substance. We first grasp the sensible properties and observable operations of substance, as is manifest in the way we speak of substance. Our intellectual knowledge must always have its principle in what is grasped by the senses; that is why our words, which signify what we understand, have the sensible as their *id a quo*.[36] But just as our knowledge is not restricted to what is grasped by the senses, so too names first imposed to signify the sensible manifestations of things can be made to signify the substance that underlies sensible accidents. When names imposed in this fashion are taken as signifying the *id a quo* rather than the *id ad quod*, they signify less properly. Thus, the word

36. "Secundum autem quod res sunt nobis notae, secundum hoc a nobis nominantur" (*In V Metaphysic.*, lect. 1, n. 751).

"life" is imposed from an effect, self-movement, a vital operation, but the term is imposed to signify the substance that has the ability to move itself, not the operation. Sometimes, however, "life" is taken to signify vital operations as such and is then said to signify less properly.[37]

The distinction, then, is clear. For the most part, we must distinguish in names between that in sense experience from which the name is taken and that which it is imposed to signify. Sometimes, as is the case with the proper objects of the senses, the *id a quo* and the *id ad quod* are the same. The distinction seems to be one between etymology and meaning. The etymology of *participare* (partake) is said to be *partem capere* (to take a part),[38] that of *principium* (principle) priority.[39] The favored example of *lapis* makes it clear that a word does not properly signify its etymology,[40] and it does it particularly well because it is, if its etymology is correct, a composite term. In *On Interpretation,* it is said of the noun that none of its parts signify separately, a claim it may seem difficult to accept when one thinks of such nouns as "breakfast." This composite term is drawn from 'break' and 'fast', each of which signifies by itself. Why does this fact not destroy Aristotle's definition of noun? St. Thomas argues that the composite term signifies a simple conception and that, although its parts taken separately signify something, they do not signify part of what the composite noun signifies. For example, "break" does not signify part of the morning meal. The composite signified by the *oratio* or sentence, on the other hand, is such that a part of the *oratio* signifies part of the composite conception. Thus, the etymology of the word does not function as do the parts of, say, a sentence. St. Thomas's example in arguing this is, again, *lapis.*[41]

37. "Quandoque tamen vita sumitur minus proprie pro operationibus vitae, a quibus nomen vitae assumitur, sicut dicit Philosophus in IX *Ethic.* quod 'vivere principaliter est sentire et intelligere'" (*ST,* Ia, q. 18, a. 2).

38. *In Boethii de heb.,* lect. 2.

39. "Dicendum quod licet hoc nomen principium, quantum ad id a quo imponitur ad significandum, videatur a prioritate sumptum: non tamen significat prioritatem, seu originem. Non enim idem est quod significat nomen, et a quo nomen imponitur . . ." (*ST,* Ia, q. 33, a. 1 ad 3).

40. Cf. *Q. D. de pot.,* q. 9, a. 3 ad 1; *ST,* IIaIIae, q. 92, a. 1 ad 2; *I Sent.,* d. 24, q. 2, a. 2 ad 2.

41. "Cuius ratio est quod nomen imponitur ad significandum unum simplicem

Thus, the distinction between the *id a quo* and the *id ad quod* seems to be one between etymology and meaning. Nevertheless, St. Thomas will sometimes say that the *id a quo* is what a name properly signifies.[42] There is no question in this text of such proper sensibles as *frigus, calor et alia huiusmodi*. Apparently, unless there is here a flat contradiction, a distinction must be made between various meanings of the phrase *id a quo* if we are to reconcile the texts involved.

As it happens, St. Thomas himself points out the necessary distinction.[43] That from which the name is imposed can be understood either from the point of view of the one imposing the name, which is the way we have hitherto considered it in opposing it to the *id ad quod,* or from the point of view of the thing, *ex parte rei*. In the latter sense, the *id a quo* is the specific difference of the thing and what the name properly signifies. *"Dicitur autem nomen imponi ab eo quod est quasi differentia constitutiva generis* (The name is said to be imposed from that which is, as it were, the constitutive difference of the genus.)"[44]

The same distinction appears if we examine what St. Thomas has to say of denomination. On the one hand, he can say, "... *denominatio proprie est secundum habitudinem accidentis ad subiectum* (Denomination is properly based on the relation of accident to subject);"[45] on the other, in many texts, he will say that *"denomi-*

---

intellectum; aliud autem est id a quo imponitur nomen ad significandum ab eo quod nomen significat: quod tamen imponitur ad significandum conceptum cuiusdam rei. Et inde est quod est pars nominis compositi, quod imponitur ad significandum conceptum simplicem, non significat partem conceptionis compositae, a qua imponitur ad significandum. Sed oratio significat ipsam conceptionem compositam: unde pars orationis significat partem conceptionis compositae" (*In I Periherm.,* lect. 4, n. 9).

42. Cf., e.g., *III Sent.,* d. 6, q. 1, a. 3.

43. *Q. D. de ver.,* q. 4, a. 1 ad 8.

44. *I Sent.,* d. 4, q. 1, a. 1. See also *Q. D. de ver.,* q. 4, a. 1 ad 8: "... nomen dicitur ab aliquo imponi dupliciter: aut ex parte imponentis nomen, aut ex parte rei cui imponitur. Ex parte autem rei nomen dicitur ab illo imponi per quod completur ratio rei quam nomen significat; et haec est differentia specifica illius rei. Et hoc est quod principaliter significatur per nomen. Sed quia differentiae essentiales sunt nobis ignotae, quandoque utimur accidentibus vel effectibus loco earum, ut VII Metaphys. dicitur; et secundum hoc nominamus rem; et sic illud quod loco differentiae essentialis sumitur, est a quo imponitur nomen *ex parte imponentis,* sicut lapis imponitur ab effectu, qui est laedere pedem. Et hoc non oportet esse principaliter significatum per nomen, sed illud loco cuius hoc ponitur."

45. *I Sent.,* d. 17, q. 1, a. 5 ad 2.

natio fit a forma, quae det speciem rei (Denomination comes from form which constitutes the species of the thing)."[46] Of course if this last remark were taken without any qualification, few things would be named by us, since the essences of things and their constitutive forms are obscure to us. Moreover, it would violate the Aristotelian maxim, embraced by Thomas, that our initial knowledge is imperfect. It is on the basis of that knowledge that we first name and talk about things. But the form from which something is denominated can be understood in a wider sense.[47]

... dicendum est quod illud a quo aliquid denominatur non oportet quod sit semper forma secundum rei naturam, sed sufficit quod significetur per modum formae, grammatice loquendo. Denominatur enim homo ab actione et ab indumento, ab aliis huiusmodi, quae realiter non sunt formae. *(Q. D. de pot.,* q. 7, a. 10 ad 8)

It should be said that that from which something is named need not always be the form according to the nature of the thing. It suffices that it be signified in the manner of form, grammatically speaking. For a man is named from his action and his clothes and other such things which are not really forms.

A thing can thus be denominated from its accidents, and even from its matter![48] That is why, in the commentary on the *Physics,* denominative predication is distinguished both from essential predication and from that which is predicated *ut inhaerens.*[49] Nevertheless, denomination can be intrinsic as well as extrinsic; but, properly speaking, 'denomination' refers to the latter.

Modus significandi and *res significata.*

The notion of the *id a quo nomen imponitur* leads to several other considerations suggested in the following text:

46. *In I Periherm,* lect. 8, n. 9; *In II de anima,* lect. 9, n. 347; *ST,* Ia, q. 33, a. 2 ad 2; ibid., q. 115, a. 2; *II Sent.,* d. 9, q. 1, a. 4.

47. *Q. D. de pot.,* q. 7, a. 10 ad 8. The significance of *grammatice loquendo* will become clear when we discuss the *qualitas nominis.*

48. Thus, to say of the table that it is wooden is to denominate it from its matter. See *In IX Metaphysic.,* lect. 6, nn. 1839–1843; *In VII Metaphysic.,* lect. 2, nn. 1287–9.

49. See *In III Physic.,* lect. 5, n. 15.

Dicendum quod in quolibet nomine est duo considerari: scilicet id a quo imponitur nomen, quod dicitur qualitas nominis, et id cui imponitur, quod dicitur substantia nominis. Et nomen proprie loquendo dicitur significare formam sive qualitatem a qua imponitur nomen; dicitur vero supponere pro eo cui imponitur. (*III Sent.*, d. 6, q. 1, a. 3)

It should be said that there are two things to consider in any name, namely, that from which the name is imposed, which is called the quality of the name, and that on which it is imposed, which is called the substance of the name. The name is said properly to signify the form or quality from which it is imposed; it is said to suppose for that on which it is imposed.

The first thing to ask about the phrase *nomen significat substantiam cum qualitate* (Ia, q. 13, a. 1 ad 3) is the meaning of *nomen*. Sometimes *nomen* has an extension comparable to that of the English 'word'. When that is the case, I have for the most part been using 'name'; at other times *nomen* has the more restricted meaning of the English 'noun'.[50] In the passage quoted just above, *nomen* has the second, more restricted meaning of a word that is other than the verb, for example. The statement is a grammatical one,[51] something that affects the meaning of 'substance' and 'quality'. These terms are not to be understood as they are in the *Categories*, where substance is that which neither exists in another nor is said of another. The grammarian, aware that accidents can function as subjects in a sentence, as that of which something else is predicated, finds that a sufficient reason for calling them substances or substantives. For him, substance is that which can be the subject of a sentence. A quality, then, would be that which modifies a subject, i.e. can be predicated of it.[52]

The "quality" of a noun is that from which the word is imposed, that which is the principle of knowing the thing named. In other words, the quality is the *id a quo ex parte rei* and is what is properly signified by the term.[53] In the noun 'man', for example, the quality

50. "Nomen dupliciter potest sumi: prout communiter significat quamlibet dictionem impositam ad signficandum aliquam rem. Et quia etiam ipsum agere vel pati est quaedam res, inde est quod est ipsa verba, inquantum nominant, idest significant agere vel pati, sub nominibus comprehendunt communiter acceptis. Nomen prout a verbo distinguitur, significat rem sub determinato modo, prout scilicet potest intelligi ut per se existens" (*In I Periherm.*, lect. 5, n. 15).

51. *I Sent.*, d. 9, q. 1, a. 2.

52. *I Sent.*, d. 22, q. 1, a. 1 ad 3.

53. *III Sent.*, d. 6, q. 1, a. 3.

of the term is human nature, and the substance is the supposit subsisting in that nature. Thomas observes that "to signify the substance with quality is to signify the supposit with the nature or determinate form in which it subsists."[54] So, too, "white" signifies that which is whiteness, whiteness being the quality, the form, by which the thing is known and from which it is named, substance being the carrier of the quality and that which is known via it. It is the form or quality, the principle of knowing the thing, that the noun principally signifies.[55]

The *id a quo ex parte rei,* the specific difference, that in virtue of which the thing is intelligible, is what the name principally signifies. The form principally signified is either the simple form of the abstract term, or the form by which the composite of the concrete term is known. It is in this context that we find the distinction made between what the word signifies (*res significata*) and its way of signifying it (*modus significandi*).

What is meant by *modus*? In the specification of a potency or habit, the object is assigned the principal role, which is why the science which has the most worthy object is called the best science. Metaphysics, since it is concerned with things higher than man and most perfect in themselves, is the science most worthy of pursuit. By contrast, natural philosophy would be low on the scale. When the way the object is grasped is considered, namely, the certitude of science, a different order of precedence appears. The most perfect science we have is not concerned with the noblest things. Indeed, the science which is first in dignity, in object, is last from the point of view of certitude and evidence, that is, of mode.[56] Just as mode presupposes science, so generally speaking any modification presupposes what it modifies and does not constitute it.[57] And so we come to what is signified and the mode of signifying.

Names signify things as they are known and not immediately as they exist. The fact that all our knowledge takes its rise from the

---

54. "Dicendum quod significare substantiam cum qualitate, est significare suppositum cum natura vel forma determinata in qua subsistit" (*ST,* Ia, q. 13, a. 1, ad 3).

55. *I Sent.,* d. 22, q. 1, a. 1 ad 3.

56. *In I De anima,* lect. 1, nn.4–5; see also *I Sent., prologus,* q. 1, a. 3, sol. 2.

57. See Cajetan, *In II Periherm.,* lect. 8, n. 3: "Quia modificare proprie dicatur aliquid, quando redditur aliquale, non quando fit secundum suam substantiam."

senses, so that the quiddity of material things is the proper object of our intellect, has an effect on the way or mode we know whatever we know—even when what we know is not the quiddity of a material thing. Because there is a difference between form and the subject of the form in the material things to which our mind is proportioned, we have one mode or way of signifying the composite of form and matter and another way of signifying the form as such. Thomas calls these the concrete and abstract modes of signification.[58] Names that signify forms do not signify them as subsisting; it is the composite that has the form that subsists.[59]

Et quia in huiusmodi creaturis, ea quae sunt perfecta et subsistentia, sunt composita; forma autem in eis non est aliquid completum subsistens, sed magis quo aliquid est: inde est quod omnia nomina a nobis imposita ad significandum aliquid completum subsistens, significant in concretione, prout competit compositis; quae imponuntur ad significandas formas simplices, significant aliquid non ut subsistens, sed ut quo aliquid est: sicut albedo significat ut quo aliquid est album. (*ST*, Ia, q. 13, a. 1 ad 2)

Because the creatures of this kind that are perfect and subsistent are composites, their form is not something complete and subsistent, but rather that whereby something is; hence all the words imposed by us to signify something complete and subsistent signify in concretion, which is proper to composites; and those imposed to signify simple forms signify something, not as subsistent, but as that whereby something is: as whiteness signifies that whereby something is white.

'Humanity' signifies human nature abstractly, not as something which subsists, but as that by which a man is a man; 'man' signifies the same nature concretely, as that which has humanity, a subsistent thing which might be encountered in the world around us. Concrete terms imply a composition of the form and a subject and for the moment it does not matter whether our examples are 'humanity' and 'man', or 'whiteness' and 'white'. Human nature is signified by 'humanity' *per modum partis*, since it is that whereby a man is a man. Many things are true of man besides what is signified by 'humanity', e.g. fat, white, etc. The abstract term is said to signify the nature with precision, that is, prescinding in its mode of signifying from everything but the essential principles of the nature signified.[60] From the

---

58. *I Summa contra gentiles*, cap. 30.
59. *ST*, Ia, q. 13, a. 1 ad 2.
60. See *Quodlib.* IX, q. 2, a. 1 ad 1: ". . . dicendum quod ex unione animae et corporis constituitur et homo et humanitas: quae quidem duo hoc modo differunt: quod *humanitas* significatur *per modum partis*, eo quod humanitas dicitur qua homo est homo, et sic praecise significat essentialia principia speciei, per quae hoc indi-

point of view of the concrete whole, man, humanity is a part. Yet humanity is what is formal in the composite, making it to be the kind of thing it is; that is why it is called the *forma totius*, not the *forma partis*.[61] The concrete term 'man' is said to signify *per modum totius* since it signifies that which has humanity without prescinding from what is not essential. Thus 'man' is predicated of Socrates whereas 'humanity' cannot be, directly (*in recto*), although 'man' does not include in its signification the accidents of such individuals as Socrates.

Unde licet in significatione hominis non includantur accidentia eius, non tamen homo significat aliquid separatum ab accidentibus; et ideo homo significat ut totum, humanitas significat ut pars. (*In Metaphysic.*, lect. 5, n. 1379)

Hence although his accidents are not included in the signification of 'man', neither does 'man' signify something separated from accidents. Therefore 'man' signifies as a whole, 'humanity' as a part.

As we shall see in chapter 9, no matter how perfect the *res* signified by a name that is attributed to God, the mode of signifying is always defective (*quantum ad modum significandi, omne nomen cum defectu est*).[62]

Ratio quam significat nomen[63]

St. Thomas adopts the theory of signification he found in Aristotle's *On Interpretation*: the word signifies the thing (*res*), not directly, but via a conception of the mind. This conception, as directly and immediately signified by the word, is given the technical logical designation, *ratio*.[64] In order to isolate the *conceptio* or *ratio*, we

---

viduum in tali specie collocatur; unde se habet per modum partis, cum praeter huiusmodi principia multa alia in rebus naturae inveniuntur. Sed *homo* significatur *per modum totius*: homo enim dicitur habens humanitatem, vel subsistens in humanitate, sine praecisione quorumcumque aliorum supervenientium essentialibus principiis speciei; quia per hoc quod dico: Habens humanitatem, non praeciditur, qui habet colorem, et quantitatem et alia huiusmodi." See also *De ente et essentia*, cap. 3 and Joseph Bobik's magisterial *Aquinas on Being and Essence* (Notre Dame, In.: Notre Dame University Press, 1965).

61. *In VII Metaphysic.*, lect. 9, nn. 1467-9.
62. *I Summa contra gentiles*, cap. 30.
63. For the phrase, a recurrent one, see *In IV Metaphysic.* lect. 16, n. 733.
64. "Ratio enim quam significat nomen, est conceptio intellectus de re significata per nomen" (*ST*, Ia, q. 13, a. 4).

note, with Thomas, that, when a man understands, he can be considered to be related to four things: to the thing understood, to the intelligible species by which the intellect is actualized, to the act of understanding, and, finally, to the conception.[65]

Quae quidem conceptio a tribus praedictis differt. *A re* quidem intellecta, quia res intellecta est interdum extra intellectum, conceptio autem intellectus non est nisi in intellectu; et iterum conceptio intellectus ordinatur ad rem intellectam sicut ad finem: propter hoc enim intellectus conceptionem rei in se format ut rem intellectam cognoscat. Differt autem *a specie* intelligibili, nam species intelligiblis qua fit intellectus in actu, considerat ut principium actionis intellectus, cum omne agens agat secundum quod est in actu; actu autem fit per aliquam formam, quam oportet esse actionis principium. Differt autem *ab actione* intellectus, quia praedicta conceptio consideratur ut terminus actionis, et quasi quoddam per ipsam constitutum. (*Q. D. de pot.,* q. 8, a. 1)

The conception differs from the foregoing three. From *the thing* understood, indeed, because the thing understood is sometimes outside intellect whereas the concept is only in the mind; moreover, the intellect's conception is ordered to the thing understood as to its end: the intellect forms a conception of the thing in itself in order to know the thing understood. It differs from the *intelligible species* whereby the intellect is actualized and is as a principle of the intellect's action, since every agent acts insofar as it is in act, and it comes to be in act through some form which must then be a principle of action. It differs from *the action* of intellect, because the aforesaid conception is considered to be the term of action and as it were constituted by it.

The conception produced by the act of understanding is what the word signifies; indeed, the conception itself is called a word.[66] The inner word is said to be both the efficient and the final cause of the spoken word. It is the final cause for the reason just given: the purpose of the spoken word is to express and signify the concept or inner word. It is the efficient cause of the spoken word "because the word which is spoken aloud, since it signifies conventionally, has will as its principle, as do other artifacts; therefore, as in the case

65. The following passage is from *Q. D. de pot.,* q. 8, a. 1; see too ibid., q. 9, a. 5.

66. "Haec autem conceptio intellectus in nobis proprie *verbum* dicitur: hoc enim est quod verbo exteriore significatur: vox enim exterior neque significat ipsum intellectum, neque speciem intelligibilem, neque actum intellectus, sed intellectus conceptionem, qua mediante refertur ad rem" (*Q. D. de pot.,* q. 8, a. 1).

of other artifacts there preexists in the mind of the artisan an image of the external artifact, so in the mind of one pronouncing a word there preexists an exemplar of the external word."[67] The conception is called the *verbum cordis* whereas as exemplar of the spoken word it is called the *verbum interius*.[68] What now is the significance of calling the conception a *ratio*?

St. Thomas gives us an extensive and exhaustive statement of what is meant by *ratio* in this regard, as well the manner of its reference to the real order. "Ratio nihil aliud est quam id quod apprehendit intellectus de significatione alicuius nominis (*ratio* is nothing else than what the intellect grasps of the signification of some name)."[69] Sometimes, but not always, the *ratio* signified by the name is a definition; we know and name many things that cannot be defined, properly speaking, notably, substance, quantity, and the other supreme genera. (Properly speaking, a definition consists of the proximate genus and specific difference.) Now if that which the word signifies is sometimes a definition, *ratio*, like definition, must be a second intention. The conception, considered as a definition, is a *secundum intellectum*, a second intention.[70] So too, in the phrase *ratio quam significat est definitio*, *ratio* is also a name of second intention. *Ratio*, of course, can mean other things,[71] but we are presently interested in it insofar as it is a *nomen intentionis*.[72] To be a *ratio* is something that happens to a thing insofar as it is

67. "Efficiens autem, quia verbum prolatum exterius, cum sit significativum ad placitum, eius principium est voluntas, sicut et ceterorum artificiatorum; et ideo, sicut aliorum artificiatorum praeexistit in mente artificis imago quaedam exterioris artificii, ita in mente proferentis verbum exterius, praeexistit quoddam exemplar exterioris verbi" (*Q. D. de ver.*, q. 4, a. 1).

68. Ibid. We might mention that St. Thomas is here presenting *verbum* as an analogous name; ad 8 gives the etymology of the term: ". . . a verberatione vel a boatu."

69. *I Sent.*, d. 2, q. 1, a. 3.

70. *Q. D. de pot.*, q. 7, a. 9: "Prima enim intellecta sunt res extra animam, in quae primo intellectus intelligenda fertur. Secunda autem intellecta dicuntur intentiones consequentes modum intelligendi: hoc enim secundo intellectus intelligit inquantum reflectitur supra se ipsum, intelligens se intelligere et modum quo intelligit."

71. See *In de divinis nominibus*, lect. 5, n. 735. 'Ratio' can mean (a) quaedam cognoscitiva virtus, (b) causa, ut, e.g., 'qua ratione hoc fecisti?', (c) computatio, (d) aliquid simplex abstractum a multis, sicut dicitur ratio hominis id quod per considerationem abstrahitur a singularibus, ad hominis naturam pertinens. It is with this last sense that we are presently concerned.

72. *I Sent.*, d. 33, q. 1, a. 1 ad 3; and *ibid.*, d. 25, q. 1, a. 1 ad 2 for "definitio."

conceived by our intellect: it is a relation following on our mode of knowing, just as species, genus, difference, and definition are.[73]

Nec tamen hoc nomen ratio significat ipsam conceptionem, quia hoc significatur per nomen rei, sed significat intentionem huius conceptionis, sicut et hoc nomen definitio, et alia nomina secundae impositionis. (*I Sent.*, d. 2, q. 1, a. 3)

This term 'ratio' does not signify the conception itself, because this is signified by the name of a thing, but it signifies the intention of this conception, just like 'definition' and other names of second imposition.

The distinction between the *nomen rei* and *nomen intentionis* is fundamental.[74] 'Man' is an example of a *nomen rei*. What does it signify? Rational animal. This is the nature grasped in the concept and verified in the real order. The term *ratio* applied to 'rational animal' signifies a *relatio* that attaches to the nature as it exists in the mind, the relation of the nature conceived to the word imposed to signify it.

This is a difficult but important doctrine. St. Thomas points out that it underlies every discussion of the divine names. The subtlety involved is apparent when we watch St. Thomas handle the question that asks if the *ratio* exists in reality. In a sense, we can say that it does, but the qualifications are significant.[75]

Non enim hoc dicitur, quasi ipsa intentio quam significat nomen rationis, sit in re; aut etiam ipsa conceptio cui convenit talis intentio, sit in re extra animam, cum sit in anima sicut in subjecto: sed dicitur esse in re, inquantum in re extra animam est aliquid quod respondet conceptioni animae, sicut significatum signo. (*I Sent.* d. 2, q. 1, a. 3)

For this is not said as if the intention that the name 'ratio' signifies is in reality, nor even that the conception to which such an intention belongs is really outside the mind, since it is in the mind as in a subject; but it is said to be in reality, insofar as there is really something outside the mind that answers to the conception of the soul, as the signified to the sign.

Notice that the nature conceived can be called the *ratio* of a given name, but what *ratio* names is the relation, or the known nature as

73. *Q. D. de pot.*, q. 7, a. 6.
74. The previous block quote is taken from *I Sent.*, d. 2, q. 1, a. 3. See too *ST*, Ia, q. 30, a. 4.
75. *I Sent.*, d. 2, q. 1, a. 3.

subject of the logical relation. The relation itself does not exist 'out there' anymore than the concept does; but the nature conceived and as such the subject of such intentions as genus, species, ratio, etc. may exist 'out there'. There are degrees of dependence on, or reference to, extramental reality in names. The concept is a sign of a real nature, and the name signifying it is called a *nomen rei* (e.g. "man"). The concept does not exist in reality outside the mind since it is precisely an accident of intellect,[76] but something in reality answers directly to it as the signified to the sign. Second intentions, on the other hand, have as their proximate foundation the nature existing in the mind, the nature as known; there is nothing in reality that answers immediately and directly to logical relations. If we add to names of first and second intentions names of fictional beings, we can distinguish with St. Thomas three ways in which names refer to reality.[77]

Insofar as we speak of the nature signified by the name as a *ratio*, we are adequately put on notice that we are engaged in a logical discussion; that is, we are considering natures, not as they exist *in rerum natura*, but from the point of view of the relations they take on as known by us. "Logicus enim considerat modum praedicandi, et non existentiam rei: the logician considers the mode of predicating and not the existence of the thing."[78] The nature as signified by the name, as well as the different ways in which words signify—univocally, equivocally, analogically—are logical considerations carried on in logical terminology.

Signification and Supposition

We have distinguished the *id a quo* that is the etymology of the word from the *id a quo* that is its quality, that is, the form principally signified by it. We must now distinguish the *id a quo* in this second

---

76. *Q. D. de pot.*, q. 8, a. 1.
77. *I Sent.*, d. 2, q. 1, a. 3.
78. *In VII Metaphys.*, lect. 17, n. 1658. See too ibid., lect. 9, n. 1460: "Dicit ergo primo quod omnis 'definitio est quaedam ratio', idest quaedam compositio nominum per rationem ordinata . . ."

sense from the supposition of the term. Supposition, like etymology, differs from the signification of the term. The need for this further distinction is made clear in the following text:[79]

> Dicendum quod in quolibet nomine est duo considerare: scilicet id a quo imponitur nomen, quod dicitur qualitas nominis, et id cui imponitur, quod dicitur substantia nominis. Et nomen, proprie loquendo, dicitur significare formam sive qualitatem a qua imponitur nomen: dicitur vero supponere pro eo cui imponitur. (*III Sent.* d. 6, q. 1, a. 3)

> It should be said that there are two things to take into account in any name, namely, that from which the name is imposed, its quality, and that on which it is imposed, its substance. Properly speaking, the name is said to signify the form or quality from which it is imposed; it is said to suppose for that on which it is imposed.

The significance of this distinction for our purposes is clear; a diversity in supposition will not give rise to equivocation.[80] Moreover, as we shall see later, metaphor is a question of supposition rather than signification. If that is so, it will be important for settling whether or not metaphor is some kind of analogous name.

In the following text,[81] Thomas compares signification with supposition and what was called *copulatio*.

> . . . propria ratio nominis est quam significat nomen, secundum Philosophum. Id autem *cui* attribuitur nomen, si sit recte sumptum sub re significata per nomen, sicut determinatum sub indeterminato, dicitur supponi per nomen; si autem non sit recte sumptum sub re nominis, dicitur copulari per nomen; sicut hoc nomen *animal* significat substantiam animatam sensibilem, et *album* significat colorem disgregativum visus; *homo* vero recte

---

79. *III Sent.*, d. 6, q. 1, a. 3.

80. ". . . aequivocatio inducitur ex diversa forma significata per nomen, non autem ex diversitate suppositionis: non enim hoc nomen homo aequivoce sumitur ex eo quod quandoque supponit pro Platone, quandoque pro Sorte" (*IV Summa contra gentiles*, cap. 49). Cf. *Compendium theologiae*, cap. 211; *Q. D. de unione verbi incarnati*, a. 2 ad 4: "Dicendum quod univocatio et aequivocatio attenditur secundum quod ratio nominis est eadem vel non eadem. Ratio autem nominis est quam significat definitio; et ideo aequivocatio et univocatio secundum significationem attenditur et non secundum supposita."

81. *Q. D. de pot.*, q. 9, a. 4; cf. *III Sent.*, d. 7, q. 1, a. 1 ad 5. In *ST*, Ia, q. 39, a. 5 ad 5, St. Thomas attributes the distinction between supposition and copulation to sophists, which is why we are excusing ourselves from discussion of *copulatio*. This is not a sanctimonious disclaimer, i.e., a denial of sophistry on my part, but a remark about its relevance to the present discussion.

sumitur sub ratione animalis, sicut determinatus sub indeterminato. Est enim homo substantia animata sensibilis tali anima, scilicet rationali; sub albo vero, quod est extra essentiam eius, non directe sumitur. Unde homo supponitur nomine animalis, copulatur vero nomine albi. (*Q. D. de pot.*, q. 9, a. 4)

According to Aristotle, the proper notion of a name is what the word means. That to which it is attributed, if it falls directly under what is signified by the term, as determinate under the indeterminate, is said to be supposed for by the name; if it does not fall directly under what the term means, it is said to be conjoined by the name. 'Animal' signifies animate sensitive substance, and 'white' signifies the color expansive of sight. Now 'man' falls directly under the meaning of animal, as the determined under the undetermined, for man is a sensible substance animated by a particular kind of soul, the rational, but he is not taken directly under 'white', which is outside his essence. So man is said to be supposed for by 'animal', and conjoined by 'white'.

Supposition presupposes the signification of the term; it points to the use made of the term to stand for what falls under its meaning as more determinate than that meaning. The species is 'supposed for' by the genus; it is directly placed under (*sup-ponere*) it. And the species supposes for the individuals, which are thus called *supposita,* supposits.[82] The suppositions of the term, its supposits, are the things it stands for, given its meaning. It seems that a term has supposition only in a proposition. Thus, in "Some animals are rational," the subject of the proposition signifies 'animate sensitive substance' and supposes for men. Such a use of a term does not constitute its meaning; its meaning must be presupposed if we are to understand the use. As used in a proposition, a term will normally suppose or stand for the things in which its *res significata* is saved. Nevertheless, a term may suppose in other ways as well.

Sometimes a word stands for itself, as in the sentence, "To run is a verb."[83]

Sed dicendum est quod in tali locutione, hoc verbum *curro* non sumitur formaliter, secundum quod eius significatio refertur ad rem, sed secundum quod materialiter significat ipsam vocem quae accipitur ut res quaedam. Et ideo tam verba quam omnes orationis partes, quando ponuntur materialiter, sumuntur in vi nominum. (*In I Perih.*, lect. 5, n. 6)

82. *ST*, Ia, q. 13, a. 10 ad 1.
83. *In I Periherm.*, lect. 5, n. 6.

It should be said that, in that locution, the word 'to run' is not taken formally, that is, as if its meaning is referred to things, but it is taken as materially signifying the term itself, taken as a kind of thing. That is why verbs and all parts of speech, when taken materially, are treated as if they were nouns.

In systematic treatments of supposition, this is called the material supposition of a term.[84] Sometimes a term is taken to stand for the nature it signifies, insofar as that nature is considered as common or universal.[85] This use of a term is called simple supposition in systematic treatises on supposition. It is clear that material and simple supposition are possible and important uses of a term, but it is equally clear that a term will normally be taken to suppose in the way we spoke of supposition at the outset, what is called personal supposition in systematic treatises. In short, "supposition" is an analogous term whose *ratio propria* is personal supposition.

These key points in St. Thomas Aquinas's doctrine of meaning enable us to go now to our chief interest, the analogy of names.

84. See John of St. Thomas, *Cursus Philosophicus*, vol. I, p. 29ff.; P. Boehner, OFM, *Medieval Logic* (Chicago: University of Chicago Press, 1952), pp. 27–51; E. A. Moody, *Truth and Consequence in Mediaeval Logic* (Amsterdam: North-Holland, 1953), pp. 18–23; J. P. Mullally, *The Summulae Logicales of Peter of Spain* (Notre Dame: University of Notre Dame Press, 1945).

85. "Unitas autem sive communitas humanae naturae non est secundum rem, sed solum secundum considerationem; unde iste terminus homo non supponit pro natura communi, nisi propter exigentiam alicuius additi, ut cum dicitur, 'homo est species'" (*ST*, Ia, q. 39, a. 4; see IIIa, q. 16, a. 7).

FOUR

ANALOGOUS NAMES

Whenever Thomas lays out what he means by a word's being analogous, he refers us to univocal and equivocal terms and notes that the analogous term can be located between these two as extremes.[1] Aristotle's discussion of equivocal and univocal terms at the outset of his *Categories* provided the point of reference for the discussion of analogous terms.

Equivocals

"Things are said to be named equivocally when, though they have a common name, the definition corresponding with the name differs for each."[2] It is, of course, the Latin translation of this sentence that influenced Thomas Aquinas. *Aequivoca dicuntur quorum solum nomen commune est, secundum nomen vero substantiae ratio diversa.*[3] To be named equivocally is not a property things possess

1. "Et iste modus communitatis medius est inter puram aequivocationem et simplicem univocationem" (*ST*, Ia, q. 13, a. 5, c.).
2. *Categories*, 1a1–2.
3. The Latin translation by Boethius continues: ". . . ut animal homo et quod

independently of our knowing and talking about them. Names attach to things insofar as they are known.[4] Doubtless this is why, in the Aristotelian definition, things are *said* to be equivocal: *dicuntur, et non sunt*.[5] If man with his distinctive mode of knowing did not exist, there would be no equivocal things—that is, things named equivocally. No one would be talking.

Things named equivocally are said to have only a name in common; as soon as we look beyond the shared name, we see diversity. The common term does not signify the same definition in each use. The English translation relies on a loose use of 'definition', something avoided by the Greek λόγος and Latin *ratio*.[6] A definition in the strict sense, one composed of a proximate genus and specific difference, is not necessarily intended by *ratio* in the definition of equivocals. If it were, the apparent purpose of speaking first of equivocals and then of univocals would be defeated. Aristotle is preparing to speak of the ten supreme genera of which "being" is said, not univocally, but equivocally. Since the supreme genera cannot have a definition in the strict sense, they could not be said to be named equivocally if *ratio* had the strict sense.

Aristotle's definition begins from things, and these things are said to be equivocal. They are not equivocal in themselves, as things,

---

pingitur. Horum enim solum nomen commune est, secundum nomen vero substantiae ratio diversa. Si quis enim assignet quid sit utrumque eorum, quo sint animalia propriam assignabit utriusque rationem." Cf. Boethius, *In Categorias Aristotelis*, PL 64, 163C.

4. *On Interpretation*, 16a3–4. We have discussed this in the previous chapter.

5. Cf. Boethius, *In Categorias Aristotelis*, PL 64, 164B: "Aequivoca, inquit, dicuntur res scilicet, quae per se ipsas aequivoce non sunt, nisi uno nomine praedicentur: quare quoniam ut aequivoca sint, ex communi vocabulo trahunt, recte ait, aequivoca dicuntur. Non enim sunt aequivoca, sed dicuntur."

6. There is a marked similarity between the various meanings of *ratio* given by St. Thomas in his commentary on the *De divinis nominibus*, lect. 5, n. 735, and those given by Boethius. "Ratio quoque multimode dicitur. Est enim ratio animae, et est ratio computandi, est ratio naturae, ipsa nimirum similitudo nascentium, est ratio quae in diffinitionibus vel descriptionibus redditur. Et quoniam generalissima genera genere carent, individua vero nulla substantiali differentia descrepant, diffinitio vero ex genere et differentia trahitur, neque generalissimorum generum, neque individuorum ulla potest diffinitio reperiri. Subalternorum vero generum, quoniam et differentias habent et genera, diffinitiones esse possunt. At vero quorum diffinitiones reddi nequeunt, illa tantum descriptionibus terminatur. Descriptio autem est, quae quamlibet rem proprie quadam proprietate designat. Sive ergo diffinitio sit, sive descriptio, utraque rationem substantiae designat" (*In Categorias Aristotelis*, PL, vol. 64, col. 166A).

but insofar as they are talked of in a certain way.[7] Nevertheless, Aristotle is not talking about equivocation but about equivocals, about things named equivocally. The *Categories* divides things, not as they exist, but as they are known and named by us. That is why it is a logical work. What is categorized is the real; categorization is logical.[8] The division is in terms of the different mode of existence (and hence of signification) that things have in our mind. Things are said to be equivocal or univocal because of what happens to them due to our mode of knowing them and talking about them.[9] This is the reason for the distinction mentioned by Cajetan[10] and John of St. Thomas,[11] though not original with them, between *aequivoca aequivocans* (the name) and *aequivoca aequivocata* (the things). Because things are equivocal as named and thus as known by us, this is a logical designation.

A difficulty can arise in understanding Aristotle's claim that equivocals have the same name. What constitutes a name as a name is the fact that it signifies something, and that something is either the *ratio* or a thing via the *ratio*. A name is the name it is, is individuated, so to say, by its meaning. How then can we speak of the

7. Joseph Owens, in his magisterial *The Doctrine of Being in the Aristotelian Metaphysics*, 3d ed. (Toronto: Pontifical Institute of Mediaeval Studies, 1978), has an extended discussion on this passage (pp. 107–135). His insistence that Aristotle's focus is on things rather than words or concepts may suggest that equivocity is a property of things *tout court*. Wherever the emphasis may lie in a given passage, equivocation requires several things, one word and diverse meanings.

8. L. DeRijk, in *The Place of the Categories in Aristotle* (Assen: Van Gorcum, 1952), vacillates between calling the work logical and calling it ontological.

9. "Et dicuntur univoca per oppositum modum ad aequivoca, res sciicet univocatae in nomine uno, ut res ipsa ad dici et ad sermonem referatur, quia aliter non esset logicum quod dicitur: quia res in se considerata, non secundum quod stat sub dictione, non ad logicum, sed ad Philosophum pertinet. Et ideo additur, *dicuntur*, et non dicitur univoca *sunt*" (St. Albert, *In praedicamenta Aristotelis*, tract. I, cap. 3). See also Cajetan, *Scripta Philosophica: Commentaria in praedicamenta Aristotelis*, ed. M. H. Laurent (Rome: Angelicum, 1939), p. 9: "Signanter quoque dixit 'dicuntur' et non 'sunt', quia rebus non convenit aequivocari ut sunt in rerum natura, sed ut sint in vocibus nostris. Aequivocari enim praesupponit vocari, quod rebus ex nobis accidit."

10. Cajetan, *op. cit.*, p. 8.

11. John of St. Thomas, *Cursus Philosophicus*, t. I, p. 478: "Sed quia non dicuntur aequivocata nisi ratione intentionis alicujus, quae dicitur aequivocatio, et haec, ut statim dicemus, non convenit rebus significatis nisi ut subsunt nomini, non vero conceptui ultimo, ideo traditur definitio per nomen, in ordine ad quod sumitur intentio aequivocationis."

same name where there are different meanings? It would seem that
we should speak of the same *vox* rather than the same name in discussing equivocals and the Latin would read "quorum solum vox
communis."

St. Albert goes into this problem at some length and suggests a
distinction between a first and a second form of the name. The physical sound, the *vox,* is what is material, and the first form specifying
it is accent, pronunciation, and, as written, letters and syllables, its
orthography. The first form adds to the mere vocal sound, modu-
lating and articulating it so that one sound differs from another. It
is thanks to this formation that the sound is a word or name, an
element of language. In this sense, Albert suggests, things named
equivocally can have the same name.[12] It is the same articulate sound
and, as written, has the same spelling. Unless the *vox* has received
this first form, it is not apt to take on the further form of signification and, since it can retain this first form even when its significations vary, we can say that the same name is retained. It is, of
course, essential to the understanding of the definition of equivocals
that the second form of the *vox,* its signification, be understood as
well. In things named equivocally, the *vox* has not only received the
first determination of accent, letters and syllables, it is also taken as
signifying. The point is that it signifies different things. Thus the
same name in one sense becomes different names in another sense
of the term. Support for this explanation of Albert can be found in
Thomas.[13]

With regard to the phrase in the definition. "secundum nomen
substantiae ratio diversa," St. Albert seems to be the only one who
has referred this to the dictum "omne nomen substantiam significat
cum qualitate."[14] The *ratio substantiae* is that which the name is
imposed to signify; the quality of the name is that *a quo nomen*

---

12. St. Albert, *op. cit.,* cap. 2.

13. John of St. Thomas (*op. cit.,* p. 579) directs our attention to *Quodlibet IV,*
q. 9, a. 2: "Manifestum est autem quod unitas vocis significativae vel diversitas non
dependet ex unitate vel diversitate rei significatae; *alioquin non esset aliquod nomen
aequivocum*: secundum hoc enim si sint diversae res, essent diversa nomina, et non
idem nomen."

14. St. Albert, *op.cit.,* cap. 2: ". . . et id quidem cui imponitur nomen est significata substantia ipsius; proprietas autem ejusdem rei sive substantiae quae afficit
imponentem dum nomen imponit, est qualitas significata per nomen."

imponitur. The substance of the name is that to which it is attributed, or that for which it supposes (what it means thanks to the meaning or *ratio* of the name).[15]

In his definition, Aristotle insists that it is according to the name that equivocals have in common that they are said to be named equivocally. Given another name, it could happen that things named equivocally would be named univocally.

Examples abound of shared names that do not get the same account.

Ducks have bills, and one should pay his bills.
Cinderella, dancing on the balls of her feet at the ball, was having a ball until she slipped on a ball.
Before he would bowl, he had to have a bowl of beer.
Can girls who can can-can?
Darn she cried and darn she did, and here are the socks to prove it.
Hail to the chief they cried, just as hail began to fall.

Language is an inexhaustible source of equivocation, and to know a language is to know that. Formal logic was once unctuously recommended as a way of overcoming the fatal ambiguity of ordinary language. But ambiguity is an ordinary, not a fatal, aspect of language, a constant source of fun and puns. And, of course, the humorless logician must first sort out all the meanings before he can assign them different symbols. In doing that he will find he already has the skill to recognize equivocation. Aristotle does not discuss equivocation as an unfortunate and removable aspect of the way we talk of things. To ignore it is productive of all kinds of strange theories. This was his complaint against Plato. There is, of course, the

15. Cf. Boethius, *op. cit.*, col. 165C: "Idem etiam in his nominibus quae de duabus rebus communiter praedicantur, si secundum nomen substantiae ratio non reddatur, potest aliquoties fieri, ut ex univocis aequivoca sint, et ex aequivocis univoca; namque homo atque equus cum secundum nomen animalis univoca sint, possunt esse aequivoca, si secundum nomen minime diffinita sint. Homo namque et equus communi nomine animalia nuncupantur, si quis ergo hominis reddat diffinitionem dicens, animal rationale mortale, et equi, animal irrationale hinnibile, diversas reddidit diffinitiones, et erunt res univocae in aequivocas permutatae. Hoc autem idcirco evenit, quod diffinitiones non secundum animalis nomen redditae sunt, quod eorum commune vocabulum est, sed secundum hominis et equi."

fallacy of equivocation, but the cure for fallacies is not the invention of an artificial language.

Univocals

"On the other hand, things are said to be named univocally which have both the name and the definition answering to the name in common."[16] Once again, Aristotle begins from the things named, and once again there is community of the name. But here, in contrast to equivocals, the community extends beyond the name to the *ratio* or definition signified by it. When a man and an ox are called animals, they have the name "animal" in common, and what is signified by the name is shared by each and, from this point of view, shared equally. Both a man and an ox are "animate sensitive substance." The term "animal" is imposed to signify what man and ox have in common with a generic community.

The elements of the definitions
   *Aristotle
      ὄνομα κοινόν
      λόγος τῆς οὐσίας
      λέγεται
      αὐτός, ἕτερος

Equivocally named = only the shared name the same, the account given of the substance different

Univocally named = shared name the same, the account given of the substance the same

   *Boethius:
      nomen commune
      ratio substantiae
      dicuntur
      diversa, eadem

   *Edghill
      common name
      definition

16. "Univoca dicuntur quorum nomen commune est, et secundum nomen eadem ratio substantiae" (*Categories,* 1a6–7).

are named
differs, is the same

  *Ackrill
name in common
definition of being
different, same

What these definitions enable us to do is to distinguish lists like:

1. Desdemona is a wife.
2. Xanthippe is a wife.
3. Lady Macbeth is a wife.

from lists like:

1. The monkey climbed the pole.
2. The cardinals elected a Pole.

and

1. There is no ace in this deck.
2. The boy stood on the burning deck.

But is the example of the *Categories,* a man and his picture, like these last two lists? There seems to be no connection whatsoever between the things called pole or deck, Whereas a man and his painting had better be alike. In fact, it would be difficult to explain what we mean by the likeness of a man without referring to the man it is like. That is why "to cow one's opponents" and "to milk a cow" may not seem as distant as pole and deck, no more than do "the miller mills" and "the crowd mills about." While these latter terms would get different accounts, they seem related nonetheless.

Boethius, therefore, introduces a distinction (166A–B) between *aequivoca a casu* and *aequivoca a consilio.* His example of the first is a proper name that happens to be shared by different individuals. The second, he says, is exemplified by the example Aristotle gives in the text. This distinction has as its consequence that the opposition at the outset of the *Categories* is not between purely equivocal terms and univocal terms but between deliberately equivocal terms and univocal terms. The significance of the distinction is this: taken as such, the discussion at the outset of the *Categories* does not give us the extremes that analogous names are midway between.

How things named equivocally and those named univocally differ is now clear. The latter have a common name, and the same *ratio* is signified by the name as it is used of each. In equivocals, on the other hand, although they have a common name, the name signifies different *rationes* as applied to them. A point of extreme importance, which warrants repetition, is that things are said to be (*dicuntur*) equivocals or univocals. In themselves, *in rerum natura,* they are neither, for in order to be univocals or equivocals they must be known and named by us. We are talking about things signified insofar as they are signified. That is why the doctrine of equivocals and univocals is called a logical one.

In the interest of exhausting the possibilities if not the patience of the reader, let us take note of the fourfold division proposed by Boethius.[17] He observes that things may be *univoca, diversivoca, multivoca,* or *aequivoca.* That is, they have one name that signifies the same *ratio*; or they have different names that signify different *rationes*; or one thing receives many names that signify the same *ratio* (what we mean by synonyms; Aristotle's *synonyma* is translated as *univoca*); or many things have one name that signifies diverse *rationes*. It is with the last, the equivocals, that analogy is located.

Analogates

We have seen that, for St. Thomas, analogy is a kind of equivocation, but, when we spoke of equivocals, we said nothing of analogy. How can room be made for analogy among things spoken of equivocally? In addressing that question, I want to look at what Boethius and Albert, and Cajetan too, have to say before turning to St. Thomas himself. They commented on the *Categories* whereas Thomas did not; but, by referring the analogy of names to the discussion of equivocals, he explicitly calls into play what Aristotle had to say about them. That is why we have been approaching Thomas via the *Categories.*

The clearest case of equivocals is had when things share a name

17. Boethius, *op. cit.,* cols. 164–5.

that gets a totally different account as said of each of them. 'Pen' said of a writing instrument and of an enclosure for pigs is used equivocally. But when a cow and a picture of a cow are both called 'animal', the notions signified by the name, while diverse, are not wholly so. Let us say that the example of 'pen' gives us a case of pure equivocation, while that of 'animal' does not. In the case of 'pen', as in the sentences given above, it seems that the same orthographic symbol just happens to be used in that way, as having several wholly unrelated meanings. Having the same name is adventitious. Asking why 'bill' is used to mean the beak of a duck and a demand for payment would not be a good research project. Demanding that we nail down the reason why 'nail' has the meanings it does may not be rewarding. There may be lost connections, of course, and they can delight us when they are ferreted out. This rediscovered link (as between a chain and a golf course) may suggest that there really are no accidents and thus no examples of pure equivocation, and that would be a great leap indeed. Consider the examples of 'ball' and 'can' above, and imagine the sentences that we might form with 'stick' and 'gum' and 'page' and on and on. While some uses may wrongly be taken to exemplify pure equivocation, it is inescapable that different meanings have been assigned to the same term without rhyme or reason, but the example Aristotle gives of equivocals does not seem one of pure equivocation. 'Animal' is not fortuitously used to speak of a cow and her portrait. True, it would not mean exactly the same thing in each use—it isn't univocal—but its meanings are not unrelated. That is why Boethius picks up from Aristotle elsewhere the distinction between chance equivocals and equivocals by design.[18]

Commentators are unanimous in seeing Aristotle's example of equivocals as other than pure equivocation. It is only fitting that it

18. *Ibid.*, col. 166: "Aequivocorum alia sunt casu, alia consilio, ut Alexander Primari filius and Alexander Magnus. Casus enim id egit, ut idem utrique nomen poneretur. Consilio vero, ea quaecumque hominum voluntate sunt posita." The use of proper names to make the point may surprise. But then we have Alexander senior and Alexander junior. On the other hand, a random selection of men named John would be unlikely to turn up an eponymous instance of the name among them. Of course, if they are all Christians and were christened John after the same saint who is put before them as a model of the Christian life, we might judge differently. But there are, of course, many Johns in the calendar of saints.

not be when we consider the purpose of the discussion as prologue to discussing the supreme genera of being. Nonetheless, Aristotle's definition can be taken to cover two types, pure equivocation and equivocation by design, depending on whether the diversity of the notions is complete or partial.[19]

Where there is only partial diversity in things named equivocally, there must also be partial sameness. The sameness is had, St. Albert notes, in this, that the name principally signifies one of the equivocals and signifies the others insofar as they refer in some way to what is principally signified. He illustrates this point with the familiar Aristotelian examples of 'being', 'medicine', and 'medical'. Furthermore, Albert uses the term "analogy" to set off intended equivocation from chance equivocation. "Et hic quidem modus vocatur multiplex dictum secundum analogiam, sive proportionem ad unum quod principaliter in nomine significatur."[20]

Not without interest is the fact that Cajetan, in his commentary on the *Categories,* says quite explicitly that analogy is a kind of equivocation. Having pointed out that *diversa* in the definition of things named equivocally should be understood as comprising both complete and partial diversity on the part of the *rationes* signified by the common name, he goes on to say that the example given by

19. St. Albert spells this out. "Quando ergo idem est nomen quantum ad ea quae sint nominis in littera et accentu: et id quod significatur in nomine, non est idem vel aeque participatum ab illis quibus nomen imponitur, nec etiam proprietas a qua impositum est omnino eadem est, quamvis forte referatur ad unum: tunc nomen est aequivocum, quia ratio substantiae cui nomen imponitur (quae est ratio substantialis a qua nomen imponitur) sic duobus modis est secundum aliquid vel simpliciter diversa: substantia enim aliqua (ut diximus) est secundum aliquid per modum quo rationi substat, cui nomen ipsum imponitur: et illius ratio diversa est quando non penitus est eadem: et adhuc a quo nomen imponitur quod est nomen qualitas, est substantialis ratio quae datur de nomine secundum illud quod nomen est. Quando ergo illa etiam non penitus est eadem, iterum ratio substantiae, hoc est, substantialis ratio nominis diversa: ita quod nihil rei cui imponitur nomen, aequaliter participant significata per nomen" (*op. cit.,* cap. 2).

20. *Ibid.* Boethius too speaks of equivocals by design as representing an *aequivocatio secundum proportionem.* Cf. *op. cit.,* col. 166: ". . . secundum proportionem, ut principium, namque principium est in numero unitas, in lineis punctum. Alia vero sunt quae ab uno descendunt . . . Alia quae ad unum referuntur . . ." It is interesting to see Boethius move easily from what might be called the proportionality of 'principle' to proportions *ad unum* and *ab uno.* It is noteworthy that Boethius distinguishes equivocation *secundum proportionem* from that *secundum similitudinem.* It is the last kind of equivocation that he feels is involved in the example given by Aristotle in the *Categories.*

Aristotle is one of "aequivocatio a consilio seu analogia."[21] It is precisely here that he promises a separate treatise on this kind of equivocation.[22] That separate treatise was to be the *De nominum analogia,* and in it analogy, which is a kind of equivocation, unaccountably becomes something metaphysical. In turning now to the texts of St. Thomas, we will find the resources to decide whether Cajetan was explaining equivocation or employing it.

Let it be recalled that St. Thomas devoted no special treatise to the question of analogous names. We have been proceeding as we have in this chapter because of Thomas's placement of analogous names between purely equivocal and univocal names. Let us then fashion a definition of analogous names, or of things named analogously, on the model of the definitions of the *Categories.*

Things are said to be named analogously when, though they have a name in common, the definitions corresponding with the name are partly the same and partly different, with one of those definitions being prior to the others.

Here is precisely how Thomas puts it:

Et iste modus communitatis medius est inter puram aequivocationem et simplicem univocationem. Neque enim in his quae analogice dicuntur, est una ratio, sicut est in univocis; nec totaliter diversa, sicut in aequivocis; sed nomen quod sic multipliciter dicitur, significat diversas proportiones ad aliquid unum; sicut *sanum,* de urina dictum, significat signum sanitatis animalis, de medicina vero dictum, significat causam eiusdem sanitatis. (*ST,* Ia, 15, 5, c.)

This type of community is midway between pure equivocation and simple univocation. In things named analogously there is neither one account, as with univocals, nor totally diverse accounts, as with equivocals. Rather a name said in many ways in this manner signifies diverse proportions to some one thing. For example, 'healthy' as said of urine signifies a sign of the health of the animal, but said of medicine it signifies the cause of the same health.

We notice that it is the *proportion* or *analogy* of secondary meanings to the primary meaning that explains Thomas's use of the term analogy to speak of common names of this type.

---

21. Cajetan, *op. cit.,* p. 10.
22. "Quot autem modis contingat variari analogiam et quomodo, nunc quum summarie loquimur, silentio pertransibimus, specialem de hoc tractatum, si Deo placuerit, cito confecturi" (*ibid.,* p. 11).

. . . in omnibus nominibus quae de pluribus analogice dicuntur, necesse est quod omnia dicantur per respectum ad unum: et ideo illud unum oportet quod ponatur in definitione omnium. Et quia ratio quam significat nomen est definitio, ut dicitur in IV *Metaphys.*, necesse est quod illud nomen per prius dicatur de eo quod ponitur in definitione aliorum, et per posterius de aliis, secundum ordinem quo appropinquant ad illud primum vel magis vel minus: sicut *sanum* quod dicitur de animali, cadit in definitione *sani* quod dicitur de medicina, quae dicitur sana inquantum causat sanitatem in animali; et in definitione *sani* quod dicitur de urina, quae dicitur sana inquantum est signum sanitatis animalis. *ST,* Ia, q. 13, a. 6, c.

In all names said analogously of many, it is necessary that all are said with respect to one and that that one be placed in the definition of all. Because the account the name signifies is a definition, as is said in *Metaphysics* IV, it is necessary that the name be said first of that which is put into the definition of the others, and secondarily of the others, in the order in which they are more or less proximate to that first thing: for example, 'healthy' as said of animal enters into the definition of 'healthy' said of medicine, which is called healthy insofar as it causes health in the animal; and in the definition of 'healthy' said of urine insofar as it is the sign of the health of the animal.

Aristotle sometimes says that 'being' is predicated equivocally of substance and the other categories; just so, Thomas notes, he will say that 'animal' is predicated equivocally of an animal and its portrait. But these are both instances of analogous name. Thomas seldom speaks of analogous names without contrasting them with equivocal and univocal names. He exemplifies pure equivocation by 'dog' said of an animal and a star.[23] He also adopts the contrast between chance equivocation and equivocation by design.[24] Unlike Boethius, he takes two men having the same proper name as as obvious case of chance equivocation.[25]

Quandoque vero secundum rationes quae partim sunt diversae et partim non diversae: diversae quidem secundum quod diversas habitudines important, unae autem secundum quod ad unum aliquid et idem istae diversae habitudines referuntur; et illud dicitur analogice praedicari, idest propor-

23. *In IV Metaphysic.*, lect. 1, n. 535; *In XI Metaphysic.*, lect. 3, n. 2197; *I Sent.*, d. 31, q. 2, a. 1 ad 2.
24. *In I Ethic.*, lect. 7, n. 95; *I Sent.*, d. 31, q. 2, a. 1 ad 2.
25. *In I Ethic.*, lect. 7, n. 95.

tionaliter, prout unumquodque secundum suam habitudinem ad illud unum refertur. (*In IV Metaphysic.*, lect. 1, n. 535)

Sometimes, however, according to accounts that are partly diverse and partly not diverse: diverse insofar as they involve diverse relations, but one insofar as these diverse relations are referred to one and the same thing; that is said to be predicated analogically, that is, proportionally, insofar as each in its own way is referred to that one thing.

Terminology

We see a technical, that is, logical, terminology emerging. We can say that the analogous name signifies a plurality of *rationes* which are related *per prius et posterius*; that is, one *ratio* is primary and presupposed by the others, this being revealed by the fact that the first *ratio* enters into the others. These secondary *rationes* signify diverse *proportions* or *analogies* to the first; they are said *per respectum ad unum*.

Question: In the favored example of 'healthy', there seems to be vacillation between saying, on the one hand, that the one thing to which all the *rationes* refer and which they all contain is 'health', and, on the other hand, that there is one meaning of 'healthy' (viz. the health of the animal) that is the per prius with respect to which, on an analogy with which, other meanings of 'healthy' are formed. Which is it?

This question is sharpened when we consider the universal rule about analogous names stated in *ST*, Ia, q. 16, a. 6: "Sed quando aliquid dicitur analogice de multis, illud invenitur *secundum propriam rationem* in uno eorum tantum, a quo alia denominantur." What is the *ratio propria, sanitas* (health) or *sanitas animalis* (healthy)? *Response*: [a] Both the abstract (health) and the concrete (healthy) term involve complexity, because the form or *res significata* is not subsistent. (cf. *ST*, Ia, q. 13, a. 1 ad 2m). The account or ratio of 'health' is 'that whereby a thing is called healthy'; the account or ratio of 'healthy' is 'that which has health'. As Thomas pointed out in the *De ente*, the form or essence is predicated of the individual only as concretely signified, never as abstractly signified.[26] The analogous term is one predicable of many things; the analogous term is a concrete term.

[b] The concrete term is a way of signifying (*modus significandi*) a form or perfection (*res significata*). The analogous name has a plurality of rationes, each of which signifies the same form or perfection (*res significata*), but in different ways. This form is the *id a quo nomen imponitur ad significandum*, that which is picked out by the word to designate the thing.

More Logical Terminology

Analogous names thus have the same *res significata* and diverse *modi significandi*. Each *ratio* involves both the *res significata* and a way of signifying it. The *ratio propria* is not the *res significata*, but the primary and controlling way of signifying the *res significata*.[27]

Thus, all of the *rationes* of the analogous name are sometimes said to refer to, to be proportioned to, the same *res significata*, but this is an elliptical way of saying that the secondary meanings are ways of signifying the *res significata*, which relates or proportions them to the primary way of signifying the form.

The *ratio propria*, therefore, is not *sanitas* but *sanum* taken as meaning *sanitas animalis*.

We see now the precise meaning of saying that the many rationes of the analogous name are partly the same and partly different. They

26. Et quia, ut dictum est, natura speciei est indeterminata respectu indiuidui sicut natura generis respectu speciei: inde est quod, sicut id quod est genus prout praedicabatur de specie implicabat in sua significatione, quamuis indistincte, totum quod determinate est in specie, ita etiam et id quod est species secundum quod praedicatur de individuo oportet quod significet totum id quod est essentialiter in indiuiduo, licet indistincte. Et hoc modo essentia speciei significatur nomine hominis, unde homo de Sorte praedicatur. Si autem significetur natura speciei cum praecisione materiae designate quo est principium induiduationis, sic se habebit per modum partis; et hoc modo significatur nomine humanitatis, humanitas enim significat id unde homo est homo [. . .] inde est quod humanitas nec de homine nec de Sorte praedicatur" (*De Ente et Essentia*, cap. 2, Sancti Thomae de Aquino, *Opera Omnia*, vol. 43, p. 373, ll. 243–67; see *In VII Metaphysic.*, lect. 5, nn. 1378–9).

27. For a dissenting view on the importance of the distinction between *modus significandi* and *res significata* for the analogy of names, see E. J. Ashworth, "Signification and Mode of Signification in Thirteenth Century Logic: A Preface to Aquinas on Analogy," *Medieval Philosophy and Theology* 1 (1991), pp. 60–61.

are the same as to the *res significata*; they differ as to the *modi significandi*.

Cajetan Revisited

Cajetan seems to have taken *ratio propria non invenitur nisi in uno* to mean that the *res significata non invenitur nisi in uno*, but the former neither affirms nor denies the latter. It is true that *sanitas* exists in only one of the analogates of *sanum*, but that is not what is meant by saying that the *ratio propria* of the name is found in only one of the analogates. It is true that *esse* is found in each of the categories of *being*: 'being' is said analogously of the supreme genera. The supreme genera are different modes of signifying *esse* that relate them to a primary way of signifying *esse*, namely as *id cui debet esse in se et non in alio*, or substance. But the categories are as well *modi essendi*; accidental being is distinct from substantial being in *esse*. This does not entail that the *ratio propria entis* is found in all of them; it is found in one alone, namely, substance.

Cajetan's error here stems from the same misunderstanding as his threefold division of analogy (i.e. analogy of names) in his *De nominum analogia*, to wit, his failure to see that the objection is based on the fallacy of the *per accidens*. 'Being' and 'healthy' receive precisely the same account insofar as they are analogous names; the few rules that Thomas gives of analogous names are equally verified of both. There are, of course, differences between the set of things analogously named 'healthy' and the set of things analogously called 'being'. There are things true of brutes that are not true of men, but that does not prevent 'animal' being predicated univocally of them.

But, you will say, those accidents (vis-à-vis the genus) are the basis for dividing the genus into species, so why not take the accidents of 'being' and 'healthy' as a basis for distinguishing types or species of analogous name? And I will reply that the logical account of how species differ from genera is precisely the same in the case of the two species: genus + specific difference. There is no comparable logical way to express '*res significata* exists in all the analogates' and '*res signficata* does not exist in all the analogates.' In any case, Cajetan denies that in a truly analogous name the rule (*ratio propria non invenitur nisi in uno*) applies. This denial leads him to conflate the definition of univocity (The *ratio propria* of the univocal name *is* found in all the univocates.) and the truly analogous name.

In short, *analoga dicuntur* just as *aequivoca dicuntur* and *univoca dicuntur*. The contrast between *dicuntur* and *sunt* must be retained in things named analogically, just as it is in things named equivocally or univocally. As such, there is nothing analogical in being a sign of something else, or in causing or sustaining it, anymore than there is anything as such equivocal about being a star and being an animal that barks. The last two are said to be equivocal (*aequivoca dicuntur*) if the same word "dog" is taken to signify them both. So, too, a thing and its cause and its sign will be analogates if the same name is imposed to signify them all. Of course, unless things were related in some way, we would not purposely impose a common name on them. Nevertheless, the question of analogy does not arise in discussing things as they exist but as they are known and named. That is why St. Thomas compares analogous names with univocal and equivocal ones. They are all three second intentions.

FIVE

KINDS OF ANALOGOUS NAME

Cajetan tells us that there are three kinds of analogous name, or perhaps four, only one of which is truly such. Others have proposed divisions of analogous names that differ from that of Cajetan, often becoming luxuriant by treating every instance of analogous name as if it were a separate type. When the question is put to the texts of St. Thomas, there is a straightforward answer. In the majority of texts, he tells us that there are two kinds of analogous name.

Quod quidem dupliciter contingit in nominibus: vel quia *multa habent proportionem ad unum,* sicut *sanum* dicitur de medicina et urina, inquantum utrumque habet ordinem et proportionem ad sanitatem animalis, cuius hoc quidem signum est, illud vero causa; vel ex eo quod *unum habet proportionem ad alterum,* sicut *sanum* dicitur de medicina et animali, inquantum medicina est causa sanitatis quae est in animali. (*ST,* Ia, q. 13, a. 5, c)

There are two ways in which names of this kind occur: either because many things have a proportion to one, as 'health' is said of medicine and urine insofar as both have an order of proportion to the health of the animal, of which the latter is a sign and the former a cause; or because one has a proportion to another, as 'healthy' is said of medicine and animal, insofar as medicine is the cause of the health which is in the animal.

We have already argued at length that Cajetan's attempt to find his threefold division of analogous names in a text of the *Sentences* commentary is mistaken. Nonetheless, there is a text in *Quaestio disputata de veritate* (q. 2, a. 11) that has suggested to some that the twofold division is, as Cajetan took it to be, a subdivision rather than a division of analogous names. Cajetan, we remember, took *plurium ad unum* and *unius ad alterum* to be a subdivision of what he called analogy of attribution, which does not properly speaking exemplify analogy. Only when we move from proportion to proportionality do we move in the direction of a true understanding of analogous names. Many who have criticized Cajetan nonetheless retain this fundamental tenet of his interpretation.

The Twofold Division

Things are said to be named analogously or analogically when they share the same name and that name receives a number of accounts as said of them, accounts that are not wholly diverse. If they are not wholly diverse, it is because they are partly alike. In what does this sameness and diversity consist? By noting that a *ratio* or account of a term cannot be just another term, since that would simply put off the evil day when we must ask for an account of *that* term, it follows that any account must be complex. The account that is the definition is composed of genus and specific difference. Any account can be described as involving what is signified and the way it is signified: the *res significata* and the *modus significandi*. Thus, the abstract and concrete terms 'white' and 'whiteness' both signify the same thing, but differently. The account of 'white' is that which has whiteness whereas the account of 'whiteness' is that whereby white things are white. Since only concrete terms are directly predicated of subjects, analogous names will be exemplified by concrete terms. The general formula for the account of a concrete term is "that which has X," where X is what is signified and "that which has" is the way it is signified.

In a pithy text, Thomas compares univocals, equivocals and analogously named things in terms of these considerations. Univocal

terms have the same *res significata* and the same way of signifying
it in all the relevant uses; equivocal terms have different *res significatae*; things are named analogously when their common name has
the same *res significata*, which is signified in different ways in each
of the accounts. That is a necessary condition of a name's being
accounted analogous, but it is not sufficient.

Not only is there a plurality of accounts when a name is used
analogously, there is an order *per prius et posterius* among them.
One of them takes precedence over the others. That precedence is
revealed by the fact that while the primary meaning can be understood without reference to the others, they presuppose it. That presupposition, Thomas writes, is clear from the fact that the first
account enters into the others. The technical term for that first, controlling account of the analogous names is *ratio propria*. All this
yields the claim that when things are named analogously, the term
is found according to its primary account or *ratio propria* in one of
them alone. Whenever things share a term and its *ratio propria*, they
are named univocally.

These reminders enable us to grasp Thomas's twofold division
of the analogous name. We notice that both medicine and urine are
said to be healthy, and we wonder how to interpret this. Are they
healthy in the same sense, univocally? That does not appear to be
the case. Reflection will reveal that this usage actually depends on
a third thing, the quality of an animal, of which urine is the sign
and medicine the cause. When several animals are said to be healthy,
we would give the same account of "healthy." It is that account that
is understood when urine and medicine are called healthy. Several
things spoken of in a certain way are being referred to a third thing,
and we understand what is being said when we grasp that reference.
When the things being talked of include something that is named
by the term in its proper sense (*ratio propria*) and something else
that is not, say, Bowser and aspirin, the sense of calling aspirin
healthy is gotten by referring it to a quality of the dog which it re-
stores.

Few readers will be brought to the edges of their chairs by such
a subdivision. Why did Thomas feel it important enough to make?
It seems exhaustive enough, to be sure, but we might feel that to

understand what is meant by the analogous name is already to grasp this division. Thomas brings it up in the course of discussing how a name can be common to God and creature. The two types of analogous name do not require any theological basis, as Thomas's examples make clear. But reasons for the application of the one type and the withholding of the other from names common to God and creature must be postponed to a later treatment.

A Text in the *Ethics*

When Cajetan describes what he calls analogy of attribution, he seeks textual corroboration for it in *Nicomachean Ethics*, Book One, Chapter 6, saying that it is a name said *ad unum* as opposed to one that is properly called *secundum analogiam*. Thomas's commentary accepts the Aristotelian distinction, needless to say, and explicates it. Furthermore, in commenting on *Metaphysics* IV,1–2, Thomas speaks of the one to which reference is made in names said in many ways variously as *in uno, ab uno, ad unum*.

The Aristotelian Text

In the *Nicomachaean Ethics*, Aristotle is in quest of 'the good for man', a 'good achievable by action'; but in Chapter 6 of Book One he pauses to consider the Universal Good in the sense of a separate form. His procedure may be described as appealing to Plato against Plato.

* Platonists do not hold that there is an idea of a class within which there is priority and posteriority; thus there is no Idea of Number as such; but good is found in each of the categories, and substance is prior to the accidents; so there ought not be an Idea of Good over and above. (1096a17–23)

* Good is like being; there is no one Idea of all that is, therefore etc.

* If there were one Idea of Good and if of that idea there could be a science, there would be one science of all good things.

* It thus looks as if there must be at least two senses of good, the good in itself and the things which participate in goodness.

But then in what way are things called good? They do not seem to be like the things that only chance to have the same name. Are goods one, then, by being derived from one good or by all contributing to one good, or are they rather one by analogy? Certainly as sight is in the body, so is reason in the soul, and so on in other case. But perhaps these subjects ought to be dismissed for the present . . . (1096b26–30)

Thomas's Commentary

Thomas sees the tacit question as bearing on the way in which the things mentioned are called goods *secundum diversas rationes*. The question is relevant because *aliquid dici de multis secundum diversas rationes dupliciter.*[1]

A. Uno modo secundum rationes omnino diversas non habentes respectum ad aliquid unum; et ista dicuntur aequivoca casu, quia scilicet casu accidit quod unum nomen unus homo imposuit uni rei et alius alii rei, ut praecipue patet in diversis hominibus eodem nomine nominatis. (ll. 173–8)

In one way according to meanings that are altogether diverse and without any relation to any one thing. These are purely equivocal because it happens by chance that the same word has been used by one person for one thing and then by someone else for another, as is plainly evident in the case of different men having the same name.

B. Alio modo unum nomen dicitur de multis secundum rationes diversas non totaliter, sed in aliquo uno convenientes.

In another way, one word is used of several things with meanings not entirely different but having some sort of common likeness.

[a] *Quandoque* quidem in hoc quod referuntur ad unum principium, sicut res aliqua dicitur militaris vel quia est instrumentum militis sicut gladius vel quia est tegumentum eius sicut lorica vel quia est vehiculum eius sicut equus.

Sometimes they agree in referring to one principle, as a thing is called military because it is a solder's weapon (like a sword), or his clothing (like a uniform), or his transportation (like a horse).

[b] *Quandoque* vero in hoc quod referuntur ad unum finem, sicut medicina dicitur sana eo quod est factiva sanitatis, diaeta vero eo quod est conservativa sanitatis, urina vero eo quod est sanitatis significativa.

1. The Latin text is from the Leonine edition, Sancti Thomae de Aquino, *Opera Omnia*, vol. 47, pp. 26–27; the English translation is revised from that made by C. I. Litzinger from the Marietti edition, Lecture VII, nn. 95–96.

Sometimes they agree in referring to one end. Thus medicine is called healthy because it produces health, diet is called healthy because it preserves health, and urine is called healthy because it is a sign of health.

[c] *Quandoque* vero secundum proportiones diversas ad idem subiectum, sicut qualitas dicitur ens quia est dispositio per se entis, id est substantiae, quantitas vero eo quod est mensura eiusdem et sic de aliis.

Sometimes the agreement is according to a different proportion to the same subject, as quality is called being because it is a disposition of being in itself, i.e. of substance, and quantity because it is a measure of substance, and so on.

[d] *Vel* secundum unam proportionem ad diversa subiecta; eandem habet proportionem visus ad corpus et intellectus ad animam; unde sicut visus est potentia organi corporalis, ita etiam intellectus est potentia animae absque participatione corporis.

Or the agreement is according to one proportion to different subjects. For instance, sight has the same proportion to the body as intellect to the soul. Hence as sight is a power of a physical organ so also is the intellect a power of the soul without the participation of the body.

Sic ergo dicit quod bonum dicitur de multis non secundum rationes penitus differentes sicut accidit in his quae sunt casu aequivoca, sed [1] in quantum omnia bona dependent ab uno primo bonitatis principio, [2] vel in quantum ordinantur ad unum finem; non enim voluit Aristotiles quod illud bonum separatum sit idea et ratio omnium bonorum, sed principium et finis.

In this fashion, therefore, he affirms that 'good' is predicated of many things not with meanings entirely different, as happens with things purely equivocal, but, [1] inasmuch as all goods depend on the first principle of goodness, [2] or as they are ordered to one end. Aristotle did not intend that the separated good be the idea and 'ratio' of all goods but their principle and end.

[3] Vel etiam dicuntur omnia bona magis secundum analogiam, id est proportionem eandem, quantum scilicet quod visus est bonum corporis et intellectus est bonum animae. Ideo autem hunc tertium modum praefert, quia accipitur secundum bonitatem inhaerentem rebus, primi autem duo modi secundum bonitatem separatam a qua non ita proprie aliquid denominatur.

[3] Or all things are called good according to an analogy, i.e., the same proportion, just as sight is the good of the body and intellect is the good of the soul. He prefers this third way because it is understood according to the goodness inherent in things. The first two ways, however, are ascribed to a separated goodness from which a thing is not so properly denominated.

4. *Explicatio Textus*

* Thomas makes a preliminarary distinction between *aequivoca casu* and a name that *dicitur de multis secundum rationes diversas non totaliter, sed in aliquo uno convenientes.*

* This second case we have learned to call the analogy of names, which is here exemplified in four cases, three of which are 'military', 'medicine' and 'being', where the one in play is respectively a cause, an end, and a subject. A fourth possibility is *una proportio* to different subjects, and it is exemplified by 'power'. That is, as sight is a power of a corporeal organ, so intellect is a power of the soul, which does not have a corporeal organ.

* These reflections are now applied to the case at hand, 'good' said of many things.

This feature of 'good' could be explained in terms of the dependence of all other good things on the first principle of goodness, or insofar as all good things are ordered to one end. Thomas suggests that this is the only way Aristotle could accept the notion of a universal good as separate: it must be God as principle and end of all things (lines 203–206). He tells us, however, that Aristotle prefers the account by way of one proportion because it concentrates on the good inherent in things, whereas the other account names good things from a separate good, and that is not as proper a way of denominating them.

Why is Aristotle so impatient with the Platonic Good? ". . . even if there is some one good that is universally predicable of goods or is capable of separate and independent existence, clearly it could not be achieved or attained by man; but we are now seeking something attainable" (1096b32–35). That is, granted that God is goodness itself and that all other good things are such because they are His effects and/or are ordered to Him as their end, this is not much help, for we are asking what is the good for man, that is, what is it that we must do in order to be perfected and fulfilled, i.e. good?

The Aristotelian objection was that good means different things in different categories, as indeed does being. We can say, then, that there is a similarity between what makes substance good, what makes quantity good, and quality, time, place, etc. There is not any one thing that is the good in each of the categories, but good is predicated in each of them, which does not so much proportion them to some one thing as involve one proportion realized in different categories.

What precisely does that mean? If we hear echoes of Boethius' commentary on the *Categories* in this passage, its ending will put us in mind of the *De hebdomadibus*. I have discussed that treatise and Thomas's commentary on it elsewhere.[2] Here let us concentrate on *Summa theologiae*, Ia, q. 5, a. 1 ad 1m.

The objector cites Boethius ("I see that in things their being good is one thing and that they are is another," Ia, q. 5, a. 1, obj. 1) as meaning that good and being are really different things. (To say that being and good are convertible is to say that whatever is is good and vice versa, that is, that they are not really different.)

Ad primum. The good and being are the same *secundum rem,* but they differ *secundum rationes.* This does not mean, however, that something is called *ens simpliciter* in the same way that it is called *bonum simpliciter.*

Being properly speaking is said of what is in act. Act is said with reference to potency. Therefore, something is called being simply insofar as it is first distinguished from what is in potency alone. This is the *esse substantiale* of the thing, and any subsequent acts make it to be only *secundum quid,* in a certain respect. E.g., a thing is not said to be *tout court* because it is white; it must be *tout court* before it can be white.

The good expresses the notion of perfected (*dicit rationem perfecti*), which is the object of appetite (*appetibile*), and it has the note of the ultimate (*dicit rationem ultimi*). *Unde id quod est ultimo perfectum, dicitur bonum simpliciter.* A thing is called good absolutely, without qualification, when it has achieved its ultimate perfection.

When a thing is said to be absolutely speaking, it is not good absolutely speaking, because it has not yet been ultimately perfected. To be, absolutely speaking, is a perfection, but it is not the complete perfection of the existent thing.

2. Ralph McInerny, *Boethius and Aquinas* (Washington: The Catholic University of America Press, 1990), pp. 161–231.

Sic ergo secundum primum esse, quod est substantiale, dicitur aliquid ens simpliciter et bonum secundum quid, idest inquantum est ens; secundum vero ultimum actum, dicitur aliquid ens secundum quid, et bonum simpliciter. (*ST,* Ia, q. 5, a. 1 ad 1m)

Thus according to primary existence something is called being absolutely and good in a certain respect; but with respect to its ultimate act it is called being in a certain respect and good absolutely.

We see here that the *unum* in the analogy of 'good' will be different from the *unum* in the analogy of 'being'. In the latter case, it is substance; in the former it is accidents.

Only after Aquinas is clear on how 'good' is analogously common to things that fall into the categories, does he ask whether *omnia sint bona bonitate divina* (q. 6, a. 4). "Sed contra est quod omnia sunt bona inquantum sunt. Sed non dicuntur omnia entia per esse divinum, sed per esse proprium. Ergo non omnia sunt bona bonitate divina, sed bonitate propria."

In the case of 'being' the one proportion is act/potency. In the case of 'good' it is 'perfectio/perfectibile'. In neither case does the *eadem proportio* preclude the *proportio unius ad alterum*. Recall that we are giving an account of how 'good' and 'being' are said of many things analogously. Indeed, in *NE* I.6 'being' is used to illustrate *ad idem subiectum*.

In the case of 'double' or 'half' we have terms that are predicated univocally of, respectively, 4/2, 8/4, 1500/750, and 2/4, 16/32 and 800/1600. That is, to speak of *una proportio ad diversa subiecta* does not in the case of an analogous term mean one and the same in every way, but rather a proportion that is realized first in one and derivatively in others. Doubtless this is why, when Thomas divides analogous names into two kinds in *ST,* I, q.13, he sees no need to go into this.

The subdistinction in I, q. 6 between, in effect, *diversas proportiones ad unum, in uno and ab uno* and *eadem proportio ad diversa subiecta* is a function of the Aristotelian text and the examples introduced. But what is to prevent us from saying that there are four types of analogy given here, *ad unum principium, ad unum finem, ad idem subiectum,* and *eadem proportio ad diversa subiecta*? Cajetan might object that the first three are subtypes of what he calls analogy of attribution, but that objection would collide with (a) the property of extrinsic denomination (understood as the nonexistence of the *res significata* in all the analogates) and (b) 'being' as an example of *ad idem subiectum*.

In sum, what has been called categorical analogy is relevant to the *Ethics*, not what has been called transcendental analogy.

Proportion and Proportionality

The text presenting the twofold division of analogous names seems emphatic and clear, but it can be objected that this twofold division is a subdivision of *proportio*, not of *proportionality*. As soon as we move away from the *Summa theologiae* to the texts that play a privileged role in Cajetan's interpretation, the clarity of the twofold division begins to fade, and one feels the attraction of Cajetan's schema. That succumbing to this attraction can be fatal has already been suggested. Does that suggestion hold up when we examine the texts?

The twofold division had the purpose of isolating names analogous *unius ad alterum* as alone applicable to names common to God and creatures.

Et hoc modo aliqua dicuntur de Deo et creaturis analogice, et non aequivoce pure. Non enim possumus nominare Deum nisi ex creaturis, ut supra dictum est. Et sic hoc quod dicitur de Deo et creaturis, dicitur secundum quod est aliquis ordo creaturae ad Deum, ut ad principium et causam in qua praeexistunt excellenter omnes rerum perfectiones. (*ST*, I, q.13, a.5)

In this way certain things are said analogically and not purely equivocally of God and creatures. Since we can only name God from creatures, as was said earlier, what is said of God and creatures is said insofar as there is some order of the creature to God, as to a principle and cause in which all the perfections of things preexist in an excellent manner.

There is no third thing to which God and creature could be referred in receiving a common name, for whatever is not a creature is God and whatever is not God is a creature.[3] But let us turn to a text that

---

3. *Q. D. de pot.*, q. 7, a. 7. This text also repeats the twofold division of analogous name: "Huius autem praedicationis duplex est modus. Unus quo aliquid praedicatur de duobus per respectum ad aliquod tertium . . . Alius modus est quo aliquid

is challenging for our interpretation, *Quaestio disputata de veritate,* q. 2, a. 11. The question is concerned with God's knowledge. Does He have it? Does He know himself? Does he know things other than himself? Does he know singulars? Does the human intellect know singulars? How about Avicenna's view on such matters? Does God know what is not? Does he know an infinity of things? Can he create an infinite number of things? And so we come to the eleventh article: Is knowledge said equivocally of God and us?

First Thomas rejects the possibility that 'science' is predicated univocally of God and creature. Things named univocally are equal in that the same account applies to both, even though they may be otherwise unequal.[4] Peter and Paul are equally man but are not thereby identical, since to be a man and to be Paul (or Peter) differ. In God, however, there is no distinction between nature or essence and existence. Thus, if *per impossible* we could formulate a notion expressive of God's knowledge, it would be identical with his existence. And, if 'knowledge' were predicated of our knowledge according to that notion, we would be one with the divine existence, that is, we would be God. Univocity, in short, would entail pantheism.

Unde dicendum est quod nec omnino univoce, nec pure aequivoce, nomen scientiae de scientia Dei et nostra praedicatur, sed secundum analogiam, quod nihil est dictu quam secundum proportionem. Convenientia autem secundum proportionem potest esse duplex: et secundum hoc duplex attenditur analogiae communitas. (*Q. D. de ver.* q. 2, a. 11, c.)

Hence it must be said that the word 'knowledge' is predicated of God's knowledge and ours, not wholly univocally, not purely equivocally, but according to analogy, which is to say nothing else than according to proportion. Similarity according to proportion, however, can be twofold, thanks to which there is a twofold community of analogy.

---

praedicatur de duobus per respectum unius ad alterum, sicut ens de substantia et quantitate."

4. His example is that of numbers. They are all called number in the same sense, as a multitude measured by unity, but of course some numbers are larger than others. The equality is *quantum ad illius nominis rationem*, the inequality *secundum esse*, insofar as *secundum nomen rei unus altero prior sit*. This seems to mean that 2 is prior to 3, where '2' and '3' are *nomina rerum*, i.e. names of particular numbers. That is, there is an inequality of species of a genus, not in terms of the generic notion, but thanks to their differences.

Whatever we know of God is known on the basis of what we know of creatures. Throughout the preceding articles, the reader is aware that Thomas is employing the term 'knowledge', whose meaning we know insofar as we understand what human knowledge is, and extending it to God. In the article we are examining, he reflects on what he has been doing. How is it that God and creature share the same name? To call this univocity runs the risk of pantheism; to call it pure equivocation is to say that our knowledge provides no basis for speaking of divine knowledge. In rejecting equivocity, Thomas is opting for a similarity of creature to God, but he does not want to overstate the case. That is the point of the subdivision of proportion.

Est enim quaedam convenientia inter ipsa quorum est ad invicem proportio, eo quod habent determinatam distantiam vel aliam habitudinem ad invicem, sicut binarius cum unitate, eo quod est eius duplum; convenientia etiam quandoque attenditur duorum ad invicem inter quae non sit proportio, sed magis similitudo duarum ad invicem proportionum, sicut senarius convenit cum quaternario ex hoc quod sicut senarius est duplum ternarii, ita quaternarius binarii. (*Q. D. de ver.* q. 2, a. 11, c.)

There is a kind of similarity where there is among things a proportion, in that they have a determinate distance or other relation between them, as two is twice one. But there can also be a similarity of two things between which there is no proportion, but rather a similarity of two proportions to one another, as six is like four in that six is twice three as four is twice two.

Thomas now suggests that we call one of the subdivisions of proportion proportion and the other proportionality, much as we sometimes call both the genus and one of its species animal, giving the opposed species a different name, man. He then proceeds to speak of two modes of analogy, that based on a proportion and that based on a proportionality, and he invokes the familiar example of 'healthy' to display proportion in the narrow sense. The other mode of analogy, that involving a proportionality, he invokes to speak of names analogically common to God and creature, names like 'knowledge'.

Do we find here a rival to the twofold division of analogous names found elsewhere? Surely not. The division of 'proportion' into proportion in a narrow sense and proportionality is effectively a subdivision of analogy *unius ad alterum*. The analogy of proportion and the analogy of proportionality are both examples of *unius ad alterum*, the first of urine to animal insofar as both are called 'healthy', the second of sight to intellect insofar as both are called 'seeing'.[5] When the term 'knowledge' is extended from sense to intellect, we have the task of showing in what way the latter is a reception of form that does not result in another instance of the type denominated by that form. That is, seeing red is not productive of another instance of redness. Grasping what redness is, the feat of mind, is understood on an analogy with sensing and the term is extended from its use in sensing, the meaning altered, so that the result is a shared name with meanings neither wholly the same nor wholly different. An analogous name.

In the text before us, Thomas introduces a distinction between words said symbolically (metaphorically) of God and those that are analogously common to God and creatures. This is a distinction we shall discuss later. Thomas's point here is that, even though names can be analogically common to God and creature, since such names must be extended from their creaturely meaning, and since there is only an imperfect similarity of creature to God, they will express at best an imperfect and defective knowledge of God. Thomas never speaks of the divine names without making this point.

In rejecting the interpretation of this text as giving us another and rival division of analogous names, I am saying that the distinction between proportion in the narrow sense and proportionality provides no basis for an alteration of the basic logical account of analogous names. That account is this. Things are named analogously when they share a name that receives several accounts and one of them is controlling or primary, a sign of which is that it enters into the other accounts. The rule expressing this is that the proper meaning of the term, its *ratio propria*, is found in only one of the analogates and the others are named with reference to, by proportion or relation to, it. The community established will be informative of the things to which the name is analogically extended according as they are related more or less closely. The extended ef-

---

5. "Quandoque vero dicitur aliquid analogice secundo modo convenientiae; sicut nomen visus dicitur de visu corporali et intellectu, eo quod sicut visus est in oculo, ita intellectus est in mente."

fort to understand what is going on when we understand entails a gradual build-up from the activities of the external senses—and the way their activities differ from mere physical occurrences—through the interior senses to the intellect. Despite the analogical extension of terms first used of lesser powers to intellect, the relation between the things of which we speak is determinate enough to yield satisfactory knowledge of intellectual knowledge.

The distance between creature and God, their ontological difference, is such that knowledge of created effects can yield only imperfect and remote knowledge of God. That is Thomas's point. It is his constant point. In making it in the *De veritate* text he is not suggesting any account other than that he had given elsewhere in terms of *unius ad alterum*. It is on the basis of the similarity of proportions—as sight is in the eye, so intellect is in the mind—that we want to speak of the latter as a kind of seeing. That is the point of the passage. No more is the observation that the one to which the others are proportioned in receiving a common name may be a subject, a principle, or an end meant to suggest that these are different types of analogous name. They are explicitly referred to as examples of analogous name.[6]

6. In the key text of *Metaphysics* IV, where Aristotle invokes his account of 'things said in many ways' to handle the community of 'being', Thomas speaks first of equivocity and univocity and then dubs the third possibility analogy, where many things share a name that refers them to one. That one thing can be an end or an efficient cause or, as is the case with 'being', a subject. "Sed tamen omne ens dicitur per respectum ad unum primum. Sed hoc primum non est finis vel efficiens *sicut in praemissis exemplis*, sed subiectum" (*In IV Metaphysic.*, lect. 1, n. 539).

METAPHOR AND ANALOGY

There seems little reason to doubt that, within the Thomist tradition, it is assumed that a metaphor is one thing, an analogous term another, and that, while metaphor is justifiable—certainly in poetry, but also if for different reasons in Scripture—it is, generally speaking, something a philosopher should take pains to avoid since it can vitiate arguments and obscure issues. St. Thomas himself often characterizes metaphor as the improper use of a term and speaks of poetry, the soul of which is metaphor, as the least informative form of discourse, *infima doctrina.*[1] When we consider texts carefully, however, the question arises whether metaphor is opposed to the analogous name or whether proper and improper usages of the kind at issue are subtypes of something more commodious that embraces them both; that is, it appears from a reading of some texts that St. Thomas does not so much oppose metaphor to analogy as

---

1. "Illud enim quod est proprium infimae doctrinae non videtur competere huic scientiae, quae inter alias tenet locum supremum, ut iam dictum est. Procedere autem per similitudines varias et repraesentationes, est proprium poeticae. Quae est infima inter omnes doctrinas. Ergo huiusmodi similitudinibus uti, non est conveniens huic scientiae" (*ST* Ia, q. 1, a. 9, obj. 1).

that he contrasts the analogous usage that is metaphorical because improper to the analogous usage that is proper. Cajetan's division of analogy of proportionality into proper and improper responds to this suggestion of St. Thomas; and, if the great commentator tends to regard metaphor as something less than a full-fledged analogy, surely that does not mean that it is in no way an analogy.[2]

It seems possible to say that the opposition between analogy and metaphor is not one between analogy and non-analogy but rather an opposition between modes of analogy. It seems equally possible to take 'metaphor' as common to the analogous term and to the metaphor opposed to it, that is, as common to proper and improper usage. This assumption can be based on the way in which Aristotle and St. Thomas speak of the extension of the term 'nature' to signify any essence whatsoever. In this context, Aristotle used the dative of *metaphora* and St. Thomas the phrase *secundum quamdam metaphoram*,[3] yet I think that no one would want to say that we are speaking metaphorically, in the sense of improperly, when we talk of the nature of the triangle, for example.

These few observations serve to indicate that the relative status of metaphor and analogy is somewhat problematic. The ἀπορία a can be tightened by recalling that Aristotle, in the *Poetics*, enumerates four species of metaphor, only one of which is κατ' ἀναλογίαν.[4] Does this mean that only one species of metaphor is in play in the foregoing considerations? If that be true, any resolution of the questions that arise as to the opposition of metaphor to analogy as proper usage would not of itself enlighten us on the nature of metaphor as such, i.e. on the genus of which the metaphor based on analogy is a species.

Although this discussion is being introduced as if it were merely a matter of clarifying alternative classifications suggested by different texts of Thomas Aquinas, it is obvious that such an effort, if seriously pursued, must inevitably go beyond the fairly superficial plane on which it first presents itself. What we are finally after is an answer to the question: "What, for Aquinas, is a metaphor?," and

2. Cf. *De nominum analogia*, cap. 3.
3. Aristotle, *Metaphysics*, V, 4, 1051a11; St. Thomas, *ad loc.*, lect. 5, n. 823.
4. *Poetics*, chap. 21, 1457b9, 16.

our way of broaching it is meant to call attention to the fact that an answer to that question requires an answer to the equally difficult question, "What, for Aquinas, is analogy?" This prelude prepares us, moreover, for the likelihood that the answer to the question about metaphor may well begin, "Metaphora autem multipliciter dicitur."

Cajetan on Metaphor

Before we turn to the texts of St. Thomas, we must first say something about Cajetan's teaching on the nature of metaphor; and, given the way the great cardinal broods over our reflections, we must say this without apology. It is well known that in the *De nominum analogia*, Cajetan links metaphor with proportionality rather than with what he calls analogy of attribution. Having explained what is meant by proportionality, Cajetan writes:

Fit autem duobus modis analogia haec: scilicet metaphorice et proprie. *Metaphorice* quidem quando nomen illud commune absolute unam habet rationem formalem, quae in uno analogatorum salvatur, et per metaphoram de alio dicitur. (*De nominum analogia*, n. 25)

This analogy comes about in two ways, namely, metaphorically and properly. *Metaphorically*, indeed, when that common name has absolutely one formal account, which is saved by one of the analogates, and is said by way of metaphor of the other.

This definition cannot be accepted as good, of course, because of the occurrence of the *definiendum* in the definition. It should be noticed, moreover, that Cajetan's failure to define metaphor is not without its impact on his attempt to define proper proportionality.

Proprie vero fit, quando nomen illud commune in utroque analogatorum absque metaphoris dicitur. (*ibid.*, n. 26)

It comes about *properly* when that common name is said of both of the analogates without metaphors.

A metaphor is had when a word is said metaphorically of something as opposed to when the word is used properly, that is, nonmetaphorically. Such lapses, so uncharacteristic of Cajetan, unfortunately characterize his writings on analogy. We might seek to help him by taking as the mark of proper usage that the *ratio propria* of the term is found in all the things of which it is said. This is a definition of univocity, however, as we saw much earlier; and, within the Cajetanian scheme, it would then be difficult to distinguish metaphor from his analogy of attribution.

In Chapter Seven of Cajetan's opusculum, we find, among further statements about metaphor, the following:

> In analogia siquidem *secundum metaphoram*, oportet unum in alterius ratione poni, non indifferenter; sed proprie sumptum, in ratione sui metaphorice sumpti claudi necesse est; quoniam impossibile est intelligere quid sit aliquid secundum metaphoram nomen, nisi cognito illo, ad cuius metaphoram dicitur. (n.75)[5]

> In analogy *according to metaphor* it is indeed necessary that one be put in the definition of the other, but not any old way. It must be included as properly taken in its notion as metaphorically taken. For it is impossible to understand what something is according to the metaphor-name without understanding that of which the metaphor is said.

As Cajetan himself points out in the following paragraph, as well as in his commentary on the *Summa theologiae*,[6] the so-called analogy of improper proportionality and analogy of attribution share

---

5. Cajetan is doubtless thinking of the following remark in *Q. D. de veritate*, q. 7, a. 2, c.: "In his quae translative dicuntur, non accipitur metaphora secundum quamcumque similitudinem, sed secundum convenientiam in illo quod est de propria ratione eius cuius nomen transfertur."

6. *In Iam*, q. 13, a. 6, n. IV: "Ad hoc breviter dicitur, quod analoga inveniuntur duobus modis. Quaedam enim signifcant *ipsos respectus* ad primum analogatum, ut patet de sano. Quaedam vero significant *fundamenta* tantum illorum respectuum; ut communiter invenitur in omnibus vere analogis, proprie et formaliter salvatis in omnibus analogatis. Propositio ergo illa universalis in antecedente assumpta, intelligenda est universaliter in primo modo analogiae: ita quod sensus est, quod in omnibus nominibus quae de pluribus analogice, idest secundum diversos respectus, dicuntur, oportet poni unum. In quaestione *de Veritate* de secundo modo analogiae dixit oppositum. Et haec responsio universalior ea quam alibi assignavimus, ex Qu. de Ver., quia ista responsio habet locum in analogis secundum proportionalitatem, metaphorice tamen dictis: in his enim etiam unum ponitur in ratione alterius."

Cajetan thus makes the universal rule of analogous names—*non salvatur secundum rationem propriam nisi in uno eorum tantum a quo alia denominantur* [*ST*, Ia, q.16, a. 6]—inapplicable to truly analogous terms and equally applicable to metaphor and analogy of attribution. He had already conjoined the last two in n. 75 of his opusculum. "Et propter hoc huiusmodi analoga prius dicuntur de his, in quibus proprie salvatur, et posterius de his, in quibus metaphorice inveniuntur, et habent in hoc affinitatem cum analogia secundum attributionem, ut patet."

this feature, which is the third condition of Cajetan's analogy of attribution.[7]

If we ask why Cajetan has multiplied entities here rather than simply identified metaphor with analogy of attribution, the answer seems to be the need for a proportionality to underlie metaphor and its absence in attribution. The text on which Cajetan relies here is, of course, *Q. D. de veritate*, q. 2, a. 11, although it is ambiguous on whether metaphor is to be counted an analogy. Consider the passage beginning "Sed tamen hoc dupliciter contingit," which occurs after the description of analogy as implying no determinate relation between things sharing a common name, and continues:

Quandoque enim illud nomen importat aliquid ex principali significatione in quo non potest attendi convenientia inter Deum et creaturam, *etiam modo praedicto*; sicut est in omnibus quae symbolice de Deo dicuntur, ut cum dicitur leo, vel sol, vel huiusmodi, quia in horum definitione cadit materia, quae Deo attribui non potest. (*Q. D. de ver.*, q. 2, a. 11, c.)

For sometimes the term implies something in its principal signification that cannot ground similarity between God and creature, *even in the foregoing way*. This is the case in all the things said of God symbolically, as when he is called lion or sun or the like, since matter, which cannot be attributed to God, enters into their definitions.

To what does "even in the foregoing way" (italics mine) refer? Does the occurrence of *attribui* in the denial mean that it is Cajetan's analogy of attribution that is being set aside? That seems unlikely, even if we were to grant the viability of Cajetan's division of analogy. What the text suggests is that a name is sometimes predicated of God on the basis of a proportionality which, because of its principal signification, argues for no similarity between God and creature, so named, with respect to the principal signification of the name, its *ratio propria*.

Does this suggestion make metaphor a kind of analogous name? Does it mean that for Aquinas, unlike Aristotle, a metaphor is always based on a proportionality? Whatever the answer to these questions, it must be said that the remarks of Cajetan we have cited are not very illuminating on the nature of metaphor. To give the great commentator his due, however, and he is after all the com-

7. *De nominum analogia*, cap. 2, n. 14.

mentator *sans pareil,* consider the definition of metaphor he gives in his commentary on the first question of the *Summa theologiae.*

In titulo, *uti metaphoris* est uti locutionibus quae non verificantur de his de quibus dicuntur, secundum propriam significationem, sed secundum aliquam similitudinem ad propria significata: ut cum dicitur quod 'Deus noster ignis consumens est', utimur metaphora; quia Deus non est vere ignis, sed se habet ad modum ignis consumentis. (*In Iam,* q. 1, a. 9)

'To use metaphors' in the title means to use locutions that are verified of the things of which they are said not according to their proper meaning, but according to some similarity to what is properly signified, as when it is said that 'Our God is a consuming fire', we use a metaphor, since God is not truly fire but acts in the manner of a consuming fire.

This is an excellent definition, as we shall be seeing, and it is free of Cajetanian accretions.

This look to Cajetan serves as an introduction to some of the problems that await us when we turn to St. Thomas. It will be noticed that if there is no formal connection between metaphor and proportionality at least one member of Cajetan's suggested division is unnecessary. Moreover, what Cajetan calls analogy of attribution would then be indistinguishable from metaphor; and, since most discussions of analogy in St. Thomas include examples that for Cajetan are examples of analogy of attribution and include no other examples, the whole matter of a distinction between metaphor and analogy is considerably obscured. Let us now turn to Thomas.

Analogy versus Metaphor

We are asking whether metaphor is a kind of analogous name or is to be distinguished from the analogous name. Some of the texts that we have examined give support to the view that metaphor is a kind of analogous name. This view seems to be corroborated by Thomas's procedure in Question 13 of the first part of the *Summa theologiae,* since in article three, when he asks if any name is said properly of God, the opposition between *proprie* and *improprie* is introduced, with the latter characterizing metaphorical usage.[8]

8. *ST* Ia, q. 13, a. 3 ad 3.

Then, in article 6, when he asks if names common to God and creatures are said first of creatures, the distinction *proprie/improprie*
seems to be a division of the analogous name.

Thomas begins with a straightforward statement of what is true
of each and every analogous term.

... in omnibus nominibus quae de pluribus analogice dicuntur, necesse
est quod omnia dicuntur per respectum ad unum: et ideo illud unum
oportet quod ponatur in definitione omnium. Et quia ratio quam significat
nomen est definitio, necesse est quod illud unum per prius dicitur de eo
quod ponitur in definitione aliorum, et per posterius de aliis, secundum
ordinem quo appropinquant ad illud primum vel magis vel minus. (*ST*, Ia,
q. 13, a. 6)

In every name said analogically of many it is necessary that all are named
with reference to that one and, therefore, that one thing must be put into
the definition of all [the others]. Since the notion signified by the name is
a definition, it is said first of all of that which is put into the definition of
the others, and secondarily of them in the order that they are more or less
near the first.

What is true of each and every analogous term is exemplified by the
old familiar, 'healthy'. Clearly 'healthy' is a good example of the
analogous name *tout court*.

Sic ergo omnia nomina quae metaphorice de Deo dicuntur, per prius de
creaturis dicuntur quam de Deo: quia dicta de Deo, nihil aliud significant
quam similitudines ad tales creaturas. Sicut enim *ridere*, dictum de prato,
nihil aliud significat quam quod pratum similiter se habet in decore cum
floret, sicut homo cum ridet, secundum similitudinem proportionis; et sic
nomen *leonis*, dictum de Deo, nihil aliud significat quam quod Deus similiter se habet ut fortiter operetur in suis operibus, sicut leo in suis. Et sic
patet quod, secundum quod dicuntur de Deo, eorum significatio definiri
non potest, nisi per illud quod de creaturis dicitur. (*ST*, Ia, q. 13, a. 6)

Thus, therefore, all names said metaphorically of God are said primarily of
creatures, not of God, because as said of God they signify only similarities
with such creatures. For just as 'to smile' said of a field means only that
the field, when it is in bloom, is beautiful in the way a man is when he
smiles, according to a similarity of proportion, so it is that the name 'lion'
as said of God signifies only that God acts bravely in his works in a way
similar to the lion in his. It is evident, therefore, that as said of God their
signification cannot be defined except through what they mean as said of
creatures.

Thomas goes on to speak of other names that are not said metaphorically of God and says that the same would be true of them if they were said of God only *causaliter.* That is, if "God is good" meant only that God is cause of the creature's goodness, then 'good' would be said first and primarily of the creature. If, however, such words signify what God is and not only what he causes, then there is a sense in which they can be said primarily of God, not of creatures. I say "in a sense" because Thomas is not abandoning the truth that we name God as we know him and we know him from creatures, so that names first applied to creatures are then applied to God. What is the sense in which names common to God and creatures are said primarily of God? With respect to the perfection signified: *quantum ad rem significatam per nomen.* God is goodness, and creatures are good insofar as they share in his goodness. What he is, they have or share in.[9]

The text just examined seems to support the view that metaphor is a kind of analogy, there are other texts in which St. Thomas opposes metaphor and analogy. In the commentary on the *Metaphysics,* he distinguishes 'potency' into analogous and equivocal modes. 'Potency' means a number of things, but this multiplicity of meanings, with respect to some modes, is a multiplicity of equivocation and, with respect to others, one of analogy.[10] The equivocal modes of potency are exemplified by the way we speak of three to the third power and of the cube as a power of the line.[11] The line is said to have the capacity or power to become a cube in the way matter is said to be potentially a thing. Notice that there is a proportionality underlying the comparison. That these equivocal modes are indeed metaphors is clear from the parallel discussion in Book Five, in commenting on which Thomas remarks, "Ostendit quomodo potentia

9. "Unde, secundum hoc, dicendum est quod quantum ad rem significatam per nomen, per prius dicuntur de Deo quam de creaturis: quia a Deo huiusmodi perfectiones in creaturas manant. Sed quantum ad impositionem nominis, per prius a nobis imponuntur creaturis, quas prius cognoscimus. Unde et modum significandi habent qui competit creaturis, ut supra dictum est" (*ST* Ia, q. 13, a. 6, c. in fine).

10. "Sed multiplicitas quantum ad quosdam modos est multiplicitas aequivocationis, sed quantum ad quosdam analogiae" (*In IX Metaphysic.*, lect. 14, n. 1773).

11. "Et propter hoc per quamdam similitudinem dicitur potens in quadratum, sicut dicitur materia potens in rem" (ibid. n. 1774).

sumatur metaphorice."[12] Why are these modes metaphorical and not analogical?

His ergo modis praetermissis, considerandum est de potentiis, quae reducuntur ad unam speciem, quia quaelibet earum est principium quoddam, et omnes potentiae sic dictae reducuntur ad aliquod principium ex quo omnes aliae dicuntur.[13] (*In IX Metaphysic.*, lect. 1, n. 1776)

Setting aside the other modes, consider those potencies that are reduced to one kind, because each of them is some kind of principle, and all principles so said are reduced to some principle with reference to which all the others deserve the name.

St. Thomas here opposes metaphor to analogous uses of a name because the latter and not the former involve a reduction to what is primarily denominated by the word in question, whereas, should it need pointing out, in the text of the *Summa* considered just above (*Ia*, q. 13, a. 6), the metaphor was not distinguished from the extension *proprie* on this basis. Or is it the manner of the reference to what is principally signified by the name that distinguishes metaphor from analogy, usage *proprie* from *improprie*? Things named metaphorically are, after all, taken to be similar to what the name properly signifies.

An *aporia* has emerged, therefore, and its resolution can only be had by determining what a metaphor is and what an analogous name is. Answers to these questions enable us to understand the apparently conflicting statements of Aquinas. What we shall be doing is looking for a way of justifying the fairly common distinction of metaphor from analogy in such a way that no appeal is made to Cajetan's division of analogy into attribution and proper proportionality.

---

12. *In V Metaphysic.*, lect. 14, n. 974.
13. *In IX Metaphysic.*, lect. 1, n. 1776. In n. 1780, Thomas gives an explicit statement of what constitutes a community of analogy. "Unde manifestum est quod in definitione harum potentiarum, quae dicuntur respectu bene agere vel pati, includuntur rationes primarum potentiarum, quae dicebantur simpliciter agere vel pati: sicut in bene agere includitur agere; et pati in id quod est bene pati. Unde manifestum est quod omnes isti modo potentiarum reducuntur ad unum primum, scilicet ad potentiam activam. Et inde patet quod haec multiplicitas non est secundum aequivocationem, sed secundum analogiam."

Ratio propria non invenitur nisi in uno

St. Thomas distinguishes metaphor from the proper use of a term; clearly we can understand the meaning of *improprie* only if the meaning of *proprie* has been established. The metaphorical use of a term does not seem to involve one of those meanings that are proportioned or referred to the principal meaning when a term is used analogically. That is, in what at least sometimes Thomas calls a *multiplicitas analogiae*, it would seem that each of the many meanings permits a proper use of the term. This may surprise since Thomas distinguished the univocal term from the analogous term by saying that, when things are named univocally, the *ratio propria* is found in each of the things so named—surely a basis for saying that the term is said *proprie* of them all—whereas when things are named analogically the proper notion is found in one of them alone (*ratio propria non invenitur nisi in uno*).[14] How can a thing be spoken of *proprie* as X when it does not save the *ratio propria* of X? That is the puzzle that led Cajetan to write his tortured commentary on the text in which our phrase occurs. In direct opposition to the text he is explaining, he maintains that in truly analogous names the *ratio propria* is found in all the analogates, relegating the rule to a type of analogy that is for him not really analogy at all.[15] On this reading, the example Thomas uses cannot exemplify what he is talking about, nor can the clearly universal rule for analogous names and the rule for univocal terms be applied to what Cajetan chooses to call true analogy.

Repeating this criticism may seem unkind, but it is essential to see that centuries of interpretation have been based on mistakes so elementary that it is almost impossible to believe that a thinker of Cajetan's stature could have made them. The proper understanding of the rule for all analogous terms not only calls radically into question his schema—which has survived almost intact, despite telling

---

14. *ST,* Ia, q. 16, a. 6.
15. "Esse ergo nomen aliquod secundum propriam rationem in uno tantum, est conditio nominum quae sunt *ad unum* aut *ab uno*, etc., et non nominum proportionaliter dictorum" (*In Iam,* q. 16, a. 6, n. IV).

partial criticism of it—but enables us to understand what Thomas means by metaphor.

Cajetan cannot accept Aquinas's description of things named analogically as such, that they all share a common name but in only one of them is found that name's proper sense (*ratio propria*), with the other meanings of the term being fashioned with reference to that which saves the proper meaning. Why does the great cardinal balk at this? Because he is thinking of all those places where Thomas says that, in names analogically common to God and creatures, the *res significata* is found in both. Obviously, if the *res significata* of a name were identical with its *ratio propria*, there would be a serious textual problem, and we could sympathize with Cajetan's effort to bring order out of seeming chaos. But as soon as the identification of *res significata* and *ratio propria* is seen to be a mistake, the whole Cajetanian project is revealed as a mistake.

Aquinas has accepted from Aristotle the view that a spoken word signifies a thing through the mediation of an intellectual concept. In order to refer to things and distinguish them from one another, we have to grasp what and how they are; talking about things implies knowledge of them. What is immediately signified by the word, therefore, is this mental grasp. What did you have in mind when you said such-and-such? There is, then a triadic explanation of significant language: word, mental grasp, thing.[16]

The first and most famous objection to this view is that there are some words whose very signification indicates that they signify nothing "out there." For example, the meaning of 'genus' is precisely a relationship among concepts, among things as they are known. Given the Porphyrian definition of genus as that which is said of many specifically different things, there are no genera out there in the world. When we speak of things as genera and species, we are not speaking of them as they exist out there. Similarly there are words like "centaur," to say nothing of "nothing."

Difficulties like this have the added advantage that they acquaint

16. In Chapter Three we discussed this at length, emphasizing that the claim that the concept is what is first and primarily signified does not entail that words thus refer to mental events. The concept is as such a concept of something and carries the meaning of the word right on to the thing-out-there—if this is a standard instance of word and there is indeed a thing-out-there.

us with Thomas's characteristic way of handling counter-examples. What has just been said is true of words or names in their first and obvious function; the triadic account fits nicely with the examples that we are likely to come up with first of all. That these are examples of the best known, the most familiar, is clear from the fact that we have a problem with logical and fictional words because they do not behave as we feel words should. They are not standard examples. They are not the first thing that would come to mind in thinking how language works. The problem then is not to scrap the triadic account but to take these counter-examples as words of a kind, more or less like the standard instance.[17] This way of dealing with the problem suggests that "word" is said of many things, only one of which saves its proper notion while the others are called words insofar as they approximate more or less to that. That is, 'word' is analogous.

Is the *res significata* that member of the triad we have called the thing-out-there? Socrates is called man, animal, substance. Do each of these terms have the same *res significata*? If the phrase meant simply the thing referred to, what Thomas would call the supposit of the term, the answer would seem to be yes. But is this the same as saying that "clothing" and "apparel" have the same *res significata*? Synonyms refer to the same thing-out-there and give the same account of it. In the case of "man" and "animal" and "substance" said of Socrates, we would not give the same account, the same *rationes*. Thus, if the *res significata* were taken to mean the thing signified, in the sense of the thing-out-there, it is the thing *as signified* in one way or another. This suggests that the *res significata* has to be seen on the side of the account rather than of the thing accounted for. 'Man', 'animal', and "'substance' do not have the same *res significata* even though they can be used to speak of the same thing-out-there.

The account or *ratio* signified by the name must always be complex. Its components are dubbed by Thomas the *res significata* and the *modus significandi*. When a definition is give as the account of a name, the complexity is that of genus and specific difference. How

17. In commenting on the *Sentences*, Thomas distinguished 'real' words from logical and fictional words (*In I Sent.*, d. 2, q. a, 2).

does this relate to the *res/modus* claim? That from which the name is imposed to signify, the formality under which the thing is grasped, is the *res*. This is why 'man', 'animal', and " 'substance' can signify different *res*.

Ratio propria and ratio communis[18]

The analogous name is one that has a plurality of accounts, with a primary one, *ratio propria*, that enters into the other accounts. This plurality of accounts is a mark of the distinction between analogous and univocal names; the latter have a single account common to all the things named by the term. Despite this distinction, we sometimes find St. Thomas speaking of the *ratio communis* of the analogous name. How can there be such a notion and, if there is, how does it relate to the *ratio propria*?

In the case of things named equivocally, we would assign the *ratio communis* to the genus and the *ratio propria* (actually *rationes propriae*) to the species. Since the proper notion is not a meaning of the generic term, this distinction between common and proper notions involves different names and not a common name. In the case of the analogous name, presumably its *ratio communis* and *ratio propria* involve the same name, with the latter suggesting a shrinking or appropriation of the common meaning of the term.

Let us consider *sanum* from this point of view. The *ratio propria* is "subject of health." 'Subject of' is a *modus significandi* which conjoined with the *res significata* constitutes the *ratio propria*. The other notions are fashioned by conjoining different modes to the same *res significata*. What then would the *ratio communis* of the analogous name 'healthy' be? Perhaps this: '_____ health'. That is, it is not so much a *ratio* as the skeleton of all the *rationes*. In the case of 'being', *ens*, the proper notion is 'that which exists of itself and not in another'. The other meanings of beings are various ways of referring to *esse* via the proper way, that is, substance. This common notion can be expressed by *habens esse and id quod habet esse*

---

18. Cf. Ralph McInerny, "The *ratio communis* of the Analogous Name," *Laval théologique et philosophique* 18 (1962), 1, pp. 9–34.

insofar as *habens* and *id quod habet* are not a determinate mode of existing but placemarkers for modes. That is, the common notion of 'being' could be expressed as "_____ exists" or "_____ existence." When it is filled in as *id cui debet esse in se et non in alio* we have the proper notion, which applies to substance.

Duns Scotus thought that, if 'being' has a common notion, when taken to mean that it can be predicated univocally, although, of course, when we formulate the notions of substance and accident, it is analogous. The trouble with this suggestion is that "exists in some way or other, we don't know how" would seem to be a disjunctive *ratio* including both substance and accident. We may not know whether something is a substance or an accident, but, if it exists, it is one or the other. Scotus has to take the framework for a *notion* as if it were a notion, but every *ratio* is composed of a mode and the *res significata*. Of course, Scotus cannot appeal simply to the *res significata* because that is not predicated of singulars.

One might also say that *habens esse* does express a mode and that it is the *ratio propria*. Then it would be said to be common only in the sense that its denominating form can enter into other notions, which, however, refer back to the proper notion. In any case, it is clear that neither Aristotle nor Thomas thought that 'being' had a common notion that could provide a means of scientific knowledge of all beings. It is just because 'being' is said in many ways but with reference to something one that substance functions as the sufficient subject of the science of being as being.

Proprie, communiter, metaphorice

We have seen Thomas making apparently conflicting remarks about metaphor. On the one hand, he speaks of the way in which the metaphorical use of a term involves reference to its proper meaning; on the other hand, he contrasts metaphorical or equivocal modes to analogical community by saying that the latter and not the former involves reference to the proper meaning. We are now in a position to state quite formally what the reference to the proper notion entails: it is a reference on the part of something named by a given word to the most familiar way of exemplifying the denominating form of the word. The question now arises: Is this or is this not a difference between metaphor and analogy or, if you prefer, between the improper and proper use of a term? Consider the following passage.

. . . per prius dicitur nomen de illo in quo salvatur tota ratio nominis perfecte, quam de illo in quo salvatur secundum quid: de hoc enim dicitur quasi per similitudinum ad in quo perfecte salvatur, quia omnia imperfecta sumuntur a perfectis. (*ST,* Ia, q. 33, a. 3, c.)

The term is said first of all of that in which the complete definition of the term is perfectly saved and not of that in which it is saved only in a certain respect: of the latter it is said as it were because of a likeness to that in which it is perfectly saved, because the imperfect is always designated from the perfect.

St. Thomas seems to be speaking of metaphor in this passage. Indeed, he continues as follows:

Et inde est quod hoc nomen *leo* per prius dicitur de animali in quo tota ratio leonis salvatur, quod proprie dicitur leo, quam de aliquo homine in quo invenitur aliquid de ratione leonis, ut puta audacia vel fortitudo. (*ST,* Ia, q. 33, a. 3, c.)

That is why this word 'lion' is said first of the animal in which the complete meaning of 'lion' is saved than of a man in whom is found something of the notion of 'lion', for example, boldness or courage.

Elsewhere[19] Thomas says that metaphor is based on a similarity "in illo quod est de propria ratione eius cuius nomen transfertur: in something of the proper notion of the thing whose name is transferred." That metaphorical usage involves such a reference to the *ratio propria,* a reference that is part and parcel of what he means by analogical signification, is also implied by the adverbial scale Aquinas often employs in speaking of the range of an analogical term. This scale sometimes goes, *propriissime, proprie, communiter;* sometimes, *proprie, minus proprie, minime proprie.*[20] At least once, when he is speaking in the second fashion, St. Thomas suggests that metaphor is simply a trailing off into impropriety because

19. *Q. D. de veritate,* q. 7, a. 2, c.
20. Cf. e.g., *ST* IaIIae, q. 22, a. 1, c.; *Q. D. de virtutibus in communi,* a. 7.

of the remoteness of its reference to the *ratio propria* of the word. "Nam tripliciter invenitur motus in operationibus animae. In quibusdam invenitur motus proprie, in quibusdam minus proprie, in quibusdam minime proprie: there are three ways in which motion is found in the operations of the soul, in some cases properly, in others less properly and in yet others least properly."[21] And then this striking remark, "Minimum autem de proprietate motus, *et nihil nisi metaphorice,* invenitur in intellectu: what is proper to motion is found least in intellect, nothing but metaphorically."[22] We might say that the thing named metaphorically is not named from the denominating form of the word but is referred to that which is so named. The thing named metaphorically does not fall within the extension of the name.

St. Thomas asks whether light is found properly in spiritual things. Before answering, he asks us to consider that a word may be taken either according to its first imposition or according to subsequent usage. For example, 'to see' is imposed to signify the activity of an external sense but we also speak of the activities of the other senses as seeing, e.g. see how warm it is, see how it tastes. And we speak of the mind's activity as a seeing. "I see what you mean." So it is with 'light.'

Nam primo quidem est institutum ad significandum id quod facit manifestationem in sensu visus, postmodum autem extensum est ad significandum omne illud quod facit manifestationem secundum quamcumque cognitionem Si ergo accipiatur nomen luminis secundum primam impositionem, metaphorice in spiritualibus dicitur, ut Ambrosius dicit. Si autem accipiatur secundum quod est in usu loquentium ad omnem manifestationem extensum sic proprie in spiritualibus dicitur. (*ST,* Ia, q. 67, a. 1)[23]

For first of all it was imposed to signify that which makes things manifest to the sense of sight, and then it was extended to signify anything that made something manifest in whatever kind of knowledge. Therefore, if the term 'light' is taken in its first imposition, it is used metaphorically of spiritual things, as Ambrose says. However, if it is taken insofar as usage has extended it to any manifestation, then it is used properly of spiritual things.

21. *In I de anima,* lect. 10, n. 157.
22. *Ibid.,* n. 160.
23. As to why sight of all the senses would be so extended, see *In I Metaphysic.,* lect. 1, nn. 5–8.

With respect to the *usus loquentium* invoked here, we must of course distinguish the mere use of a word—surely metaphor is a use—from usage in the sense of regularity and convention that brings about an extension in the very meaning of a word.[24] Without such an extension of meaning, brought about by repeated use, the use would be metaphorical. He elaborates this in a parallel text where he begins by distinguishing metaphor and analogy. Ambrose and Denis maintain that 'light' is used only metaphorically of spiritual things, and this seems right "because nothing per se sensible belongs to spiritual things except metaphorically, for though something can be analogically common to spiritual things, something per se sensible cannot.[25] On this basis, 'light' is said of spiritual things "either equivocally or metaphorically." It is instructive to see how Thomas expresses the common ground between Ambrose and Denis, on the one hand, and, on the other, Augustine, who held that light is found properly in spiritual things.

Sciendum tamen quod transferuntur corporalia in spiritualia per quamdam similitudinem, quae quidem est similitudo proportionabilitatis; et hanc similitudinem oportet reducere in aliquam communitatem univocationis vel analogiae; et sic est in proposito: dicitur enim lux in spiritualibus illud quod ita se habet ad manifestationem intellectivam sicut se habet lux corporalis ad manifestationem sensitivam. Manifestatio autem verius est in spiritualibus; et quantum ad hoc, verum est dictum Augustini ... quod lux verius est in spiritualibus quam in corporalibus, *non secundum propriam rationem, sed secundum rationem manifestationis.* (*II Sent.*, d. 13, q. 1, a. 2.)

Note that the bodily is transferred to the spiritual on the basis of a similitude of proportionality, but this similitude must be reduced to one of either univocation or of analogy; so it is in the present instance. In spiritual things, that is called light which is related to intellectual manifestation as corporeal light is to sensitive manifestation. But manifestation is found more truly in spiritual things, and because of this Augustine is right in saying that light is more truly found in spiritual than in corporeal things—not according to the proper meaning of 'light,' but according to the meaning of manifestation.

If *lux* had only a *ratio propria*, it is used metaphorically of what does not verify or save that notion. However, if we attend to the *res*

---

24. For this distinction between mere use and meaning, see *ST*, Ia, q. 29, a. 4, c.
25. *II Sent.*, d. 13, q. 1, a. 2; see too *In Ioannem*, cap. 1, lect. 3, n. 96.

significata, the denominating form, manifestation, it is possible to fashion a *ratio communis,* "whatever makes manifest" and then any mode of manifestation can be named properly (though analogically) by the term lux. In order to grasp these extended meanings, we must have recourse to the proper notion, but these extended meanings are other denominations from the *res significata* that entered into the proper notion. This is the *similitudo analogiae* that is distinguished from the *similitudo proportionabilitatis.*[26]

We are now on the threshold of discovering the peculiar way in which metaphor involves a reference to the proper notion of the word, a way that does not amount to a different mode of signifying the same *res significata.* Notice how St. Thomas expresses himself in the following text.

Ea quae proprie de ipso (i.e., de Deo) dicuntur, vere in eo sunt; sed ea quae metaphorice dicuntur de eo per similitudinem proportionabilitatis ad effectum aliquem, sicut ignis Deuter. IV, eo quod sicut ignis se habet ad consumptionem contrarii, ita Deus ad consumendum requitiam. (*I Sent.,* d. 45, q. 1, a. 4)[27]

What is properly said of Him is truly in Him, but the things that are said metaphorically of Him are said because of a similarity of proportionality to some effect, like fire, in Deuteronomy, because as fire is to the doing away of its contrary, so God is to doing away with iniquity.

Here there is no similarity of nature, or in that from which the name is imposed to signify; rather, the thing named metaphorically has a property or effect similar to an effect or property of that which the term properly signifies. As fire burns away defacement, so God gets rid of evil. As the lion acts boldly, so too does Christ. Obviously, no metaphor is involved in saying that a man is bold; it is calling him a lion that is metaphorical and the word is not transferred because of a new way of signifying the *res significata.* Boldness may be a trait or property of the lion but it is not his denominating form.

26. See Bernard Montagnes, O.P., *La doctrine de l'analogie de l'être d'après saint Thomas d'Aquin* (Louvain: Nauwelaerts, 1963), p. 75, n. 21.

27. See M. T.-L. Penido, *Le rôle de l'analogie en théologie dogmatique* (Paris: Vrin, 1931), pp. 98–108.

Concluding Summary

By way of summary we can now say (1) how metaphor is opposed to analogy; (2) how analogy is a kind of metaphor, and (3) how metaphor is a kind of analogy.

1. A metaphor consists in the application of the name of one thing to another. That is why the metaphorical use of a term entails a reference to what saves the proper meaning of the term. If we speak of explanation as casting light on a subject, what we say depends for its intelligibility on our listener's knowing what light is. e.g. the sun, a desk lamp. It is that meaning that enables us to say that something like light is operative in understanding because it has an effect similar to light in the proper sense.[28] In the metaphorical use, it is not the denominating form of 'light' that comes into play but an effect of what is denominated from that form. The analogous name, as opposed to a metaphorical use, involves a new way in which something is denominated from the denominating form, a new account or *ratio*. As analogous, it is denominated from the form, not *per prius,* but with reference to what is first of all denominated by it, the extended meaning depending on the proper meaning (*ratio propria*). In analogical signification there is the same *res significata* and different modes of signifying, one of which is primary, *per prius,* more familiar, and proper. The rule that in things named analogically *ratio propria non invenitur nisi in uno* is universal; it is as true of the divine names as it is of 'being' and 'health'. In analogy, though not in a metaphorical use, there is an extension of the meaning of the word, the formation of another *ratio.* The new account, like the ratio *propria,* will contain the *res significata,* but the mode of signifying it will vary. It was because Augustine said that the *res significata* of 'light' had acquired a variety of *modi significandi* that he was able to say that the term is used properly of spiritual things. Metaphorical use does not involve a new way of signifying the same form; the metaphor refers the

28. ". . . effectus qui est signum alicuius secundum proprietatem in uno est signum eiusdem secundum similitudinem in altero, in omnibus quae metaphorice dicuntur" (*I Sent.*, d. 45, q. 1, a. 4, ad 2m).

thing so named to that which saves the *ratio propria* because of a similarity of effects or properties. There is, then, a formal distinction between metaphorical use and analogous name.

2. Although there is a formal distinction between metaphor and analogy, we can speak of analogy as a kind of metaphor. To do so we must of course back off from the proper meaning of metaphorical use given in the preceding paragraph and turn rather to the etymology of *metapherein* and *transferre*, to carry across, to carry over. Both metaphor in the proper sense and the analogous extension of meaning involve the transfer of a word from a more usual and familiar context to another. This would seem to be what Thomas has in mind when he says that the extension of the term 'nature' to mean any essence whatever is by metaphor.[29] But surely this is an analogical extension of the meaning of the word. It could be said that the recognition of the analogical extension of a word implies that the term had first been used metaphorically in the narrow sense. Reflection on the metaphor could suggest that more than a similarity of effects is present but also a new way of being denominated from the form of the word as well. Thus metaphor in the narrow sense could be said to give way to analogy, but the analogy then recognized could still be called a metaphor in the sense of a transfer of the name, or a broad sense of metaphor. In short 'metaphor' is a generic term covering metaphor and analogy in their proper senses as developed in the preceding paragraph.

Both Aristotle and Thomas, who maintain that sensible things are the connatural objects of our intellect and the means whereby we know whatever else we know, see an unavoidable fittingness in our use of the names we impose to signify material things to speak of any other entities we come to know. This is clear from the language of psychology as well as in attempts to speak of God. As our knowledge of other entities is dependent on our knowledge of sensible things, so the process of naming will reflect the trajectory of our knowledge.

3. Can we say that metaphorical use is a kind of analogy? There is certainly no doubt that metaphorical use is often based on pro-

---

29. *In V Metaphysic.*, lect. 5, n. 823.

portional similitude. Aristotle, in the *Poetics,* Chapter 21 (1457b9, 16), mentions a species of metaphor that is κατ' ἀναλογίαν, according to analogy. Thomas seems always to link metaphor with proportional similitude. That is the only kind of metaphor that could be involved in speaking of God; the other three species of metaphor listed by Aristotle involve the genus/species relation. It goes without saying that such a proportional similitude is not the analogous name. If the cup is to Dionysus what the shield is to Ares, we have a proportional similarity but there is not yet a question of either metaphor or analogy of names. It is when the cup of Dionysus is spoken of as his shield, that on the basis of that proportional similitude the matter of metaphor arises. If analogy is mentioned in speaking of such a metaphor, we can see that the reference is to the proportional similitude on which the metaphorical use is based and not to analogous naming.

There is another way in which the metaphor might be called an analogy, this time in the sense of an analogous name. In the adverbial scale we spoke of earlier, St. Thomas recognizes a gradation in the manner of signifying the *res significata* of the common name ranging from *propriissime* through *proprie* to *communiter. Communiter* and *minime proprie* seem sometimes to be equated with *metaphorice,* and the suggestion seems to be that the metaphor differs from analogical extension of the meaning only in degree and not in kind. There are several possible reasons for this suggestion. One is that such a distance has been traversed from the *ratio propria* that reference to it is almost lost and the word seems to function equivocally. Another reason would be that there is involved in metaphorical use a reference to the *ratio propria,* even though this is a different reference from that involved in the analogical extension of the name.

Let this suffice for our discussion of metaphor and analogy.

SEVEN

ANALOGY IS ANALOGOUS

One of the weaknesses of Cajetan's presentation of analogous names is that he begins by saying that there are several kinds of analogous name. This is manifestly a weakness of the kind Socrates loved to exploit, *if* the various kinds of analogous name are species of a genus. But it is this that Cajetan wishes to deny. He is confronted, as he thinks, with an abuse of terminology. Latins are using Greek loan words in confusing ways. They—St. Thomas included, needless to say—speak of words that are equivocal *ab uno* or *ad unum* or *in uno,* as if they were analogous names. Cajetan says that they are not, not really, and the exclusion, as we saw in Chapter 2, reposes on Aristotelian usage. In the very passage in which we find the three kinds of deliberate equivocation just mentioned, Aristotle goes on to speak, and by way of contrast, of analogy. Despite the usage he laments, Cajetan seems to be saying that the Latins have made 'analogous name' equivocal. Analogy of attribution is no more really an analogy than the inequality of the species of a genus makes the generic name analogous.

I recall all this to support the view that Cajetan does not seem to be saying that the 'analogous name' is an analogous term. But is this all that clear? After all, Cajetan does introduce a gradation suggestive of *per prius et posterius* into his classification. That is why he begins with the 'analogy of inequality', the way species of a genus seem ordered despite the fact that they share the generic term equally. *Omnia animalia aequaliter sunt animal, sed non aequalia animalia.* To say that the generic name is really analogous would be to identify univocity and analogy. When he then takes up 'analogy of attribution', it is with a suggestion that, while not yet truly analogy, it is more so than 'analogy of inequality'. He turns finally to 'analogy of proportionality', which is truly analogy. But not quite. We must distinguish proper from improper proportionality. The latter, metaphor, is not analogy in the fully approved sense. Is it less abusively called analogy than analogy of attribution?

Cajetan's schema invites such questions. If he himself did not explicitly ask how 'analogy' is shared by the three or four members of his division, the reason may well be that in order to hold that they are analogously analogy he would have had to employ what he calls analogy of attribution to make his point, a *plurium ad unum*. This would put him in the unenviable position of using 'analogy' abusively when he says that 'analogy' is analogous.

If the question as to whether 'analogy' itself is an analogous term were of interest only as a heuristic device to maneuver through the Cajetanian division, one who is skeptical about the value of that division would find the question of diminished interest. But the remark is often encountered when analogy in St. Thomas is under discussion. When other texts collide with the texts on which one has elevated an interpretation, or when the chosen texts themselves prove resistant to understanding, the observation that, well, 'analogy' is analogous, has the look of throwing in the sponge. The sense is that, try as we will, no unified and internally consistent account of what Thomas means by analogous names is possible. To ask at this point what 'analogy' means in the claim that 'analogy' is analogous can be dangerous to one's mental health.

Nonetheless, the question is important. 'Analogy' is indeed an analogous term for St. Thomas. Seeing that and how it is so obviates many of the recurrent difficulties in explaining what he has written. It scarcely need be said, at this point of our inquiry, that to claim that 'analogy' is analogous must be susceptible of a clear account. It is not a despairing cry from one who has given up the hope that there is a clear answer to what Thomas Aquinas means by analogy. At least it need not be. It should not be. It is the simple truth which, far from obscuring the question of analogy, casts a welcome explanatory light upon it.

To query Thomas in his own manner on this point leads to this statement of the problem. When the term 'analogy' is found here and there in the texts, can all these occurrences be reduced to univocity? Or are we faced with pure equivocation? Or is it perhaps that the term 'analogy' is itself used analogously?

It is a simple matter to show that Thomas does not use 'analogy' univocally. The way in which 'healthy' is common to animal, medicine, and urine involves an analogy or proportion of some meanings to a principal meaning. The relation of 4 to 2 is a proportion or analogy, and the relation of 4 : 2 :: 8 : 4 is a similarity of proportions or analogies. Again, Thomas adopts the claim of Aristotle that prime matter is known by an analogy. Any effort to assign a single unvarying meaning to 'analogy' such that the term is shared equally by all these will end in failure. "Analogy" is not a univocal term.

To say that there is pure equivocation is tempting. The unease one feels at the prospect of unifying these various usages evaporates with this possibility. The solution is simply to acquaint ourselves with the different meanings and uses and not ask what they have in common besides the orthographic symbol. But militating against this solution is Thomas's way of suggesting that talk about 4 : 2 as a proportion casts light on the way one meaning of a common term is proportioned to its chief meaning. Things named equivocally do not cast light on one another in that way. "Analogy" is not a purely equivocal term.

If the answers Thomas employs in such cases exhaust the possibilities, the conclusion is inescapable. 'Analogy' is an analogous term. Given what we have come to understand about Thomas's doctrine, this is a precise claim, not a vague one. We are not likely to be distracted at this point by wondering what kind of analogous name 'analogy' is when we say that it is an analogous name. We know that there are only two kinds of analogous name recognized by Thomas and that we are confronted with a *plurium ad unum*. The first question to be asked, accordingly, is what is the *ratio propria* of 'analogy'?[1]

... dicendum quod proportio dicitur dupliciter. Uno modo, certa habitudo unius quantitatis ad alteram; secundum quod duplum, triplum et aequale sunt species proportionis. Alio modo, quaelibet habitudo unius ad alterum proportio dicitur. Et sic potest esse proportio creaturae ad Deum, inquantum se habet ad ipsum ut effectus ad causam, et ut potentia ad actum. Et secundum hoc, intellectus creatus proportionatus esse potest ad cognoscendum Deum. (*ST*, Ia. 12. 1. 4m.)

Proportion, it should be noted, is used in two ways. In one way, to mean a certain relation of one quantity to another, insofar as double, triple and equal are species of proportion. In another way, any relation of one thing to another is called a proportion. And thus there can be a proportion of creature to God, insofar as it is related to Him as effect to cause and as potency to act. Because of this, the created intellect can be proportioned to know God.

This text makes it clear that the controlling meaning of the term is drawn from mathematics. The fifth book of Euclid provides a treatment on proportionals in this primary sense of the term. They involve a fixed relation of one quantity to another: not just less than or greater than, but double, half, triple, equal.

The term 'proportion' is then extended from a fixed quantitative relation to any relation of one thing to another. In the example given in the text, it is the relation of creature to God. The effect has a relation of dependence on its cause. This is a real relation, something out there, ontological. It is the ontological dependence of creature on God that enables the human mind, from knowing the creature as effect, to be cognitively proportioned to God the creator.

We have here three senses of the term 'analogy' or 'proportion'.

---

1. There is an elegant passage in Boethius's commentary on the *Categories* of Aristotle in which he discusses the account of things named equivocally. The definition, recall, is *Aequivoca dicuntur quorum solum nomen commune est, secundum nomen vero ratio diversa* ... Boethius clarifies the definition by showing that equivocation can be exemplified in each element of its definition, *nomen, solum, commune, ratio*. Far from obscuring the definition, this analysis clarifies it wonderfully. If the terms that make up the definition of equivocation are used in a plurality of unrelated ways, it is imperative that we know which of those meanings is operative in the definition (*In Categorias Aristotelis*, PL 64, cols. 164–165).

First, a determinate quantitative relation; second, an ontological relation of one thing to another, exemplified by the creature's relation of dependence on the Creator; third, the proportion of intellect to its object. None of these meanings tells us what is meant by saying that 'analogy' is an analogous name. We know, of course, what is meant by an analogous name; it is the proportion or analogy of secondary meanings to a common term's primary meaning. This sense of 'analogy' extends the term far beyond the initial and primary quantitative meaning, and beyond the ontological and epistemological relations it is subsequently taken to mean. In short, in order to explain what is meant by saying that 'analogy' is analogous, we have to appeal to an extended and secondary meaning of the term. The analogy of names, then, is not the *ratio propria* of the term 'analogy'. It is a secondary meaning. but it is the meaning understood when "analogy" is said to be analogous.

EIGHT

ANALOGY AND DISCOVERY

One of the benefits of achieving clarity about the claim that 'analogy' itself is an analogous term is that we see that only one of the meanings of the term refers to analogous names. It follows that there is something quixotic in trying to make those other meanings of 'analogy' part of an interpretation of what Thomas means by analogous names. The primary meaning of 'analogy' or 'proportion' has nothing to do with analogous naming; it signifies a determinate relation of one quantity to another. It would be an obvious mistake to try to make this a kind of analogous name. It would be equally mistaken to try to make the analogy or proportion of effect to cause a kind of analogous name. There are other meanings and uses of 'analogy' that must be distinguished from analogous naming, and we shall look at some of them in this chapter and the next.

In this chapter, we shall be looking at knowledge from or by analogy, not exhaustively, but sufficiently to distinguish it from analogous naming. Although language expresses knowledge—we name as we know—the kind of knowledge that is expressed by analogous names does not seem to be inferential, as if an analogous name tracked a series of arguments or discoveries. 'Healthy' as common to animal, food, and urine is understood without any suggestion that one or the other of these analogates is grounds for knowing the others, in the sense of discovering them.

Would we say, for example, that we understand what it means to call food healthy on an analogy with knowing what it means to call an animal healthy? In some sense, surely yes, in that we must invoke the latter in order to explain the former. This is to know a relation or a proportion of one thing to another, but is it to know *from* a relation or proportion?

Knowledge from Analogy

If the privileged example of an analogous name does not seem to suggest a device for discovery, there are instances in Aristotle and Thomas in which an analogy is a device for discovering something, where to say that one knows something on the basis of an analogy has a quite specific meaning. We find this in Aristotle's discussion of justice in Book Five of the *Nicomachean Ethics*.

The Mean of Justice

If the unjust is a kind of inequality, the just must consist in equality—a mean between the more or less, since the unjust can be on the side of too much or too little.

If then the unjust is unequal, the just is equal, as all men suppose it to be be, even apart from argument. And since the equal is intermediate, the just will be an intermediate. Now equality implies at least two things. The just, then, must be both intermediate and equal and relative (i.e. for certain persons). (*Nicomachaean Ethics*, V, 3, 1131a12–16)

That is, there are two persons and two things, and the just is the establishment of an equality. The just involves four terms: "for the persons for whom it is in fact just are two, and the things in which it is manifested, the objects distributed, are two" (1131a19–20). Person : person :: thing : thing. The just is established in a proportionality.

. . . proportionalitas nihil aliud est quam aequalitas proportionis; cum scilicet aequalem proportionem habet hoc ad hoc, et illud ad illud. Proportio autem nihil est aliud quam habitudo unius quantitatis ad aliam. Quantitas autem habet rationem mensurae: quae primo quidem invenitur in unitate numerali, et exinde derivatur ad omne genus quantitatis ... (*In V Ethics*, 5, 939)

Proportionality is nothing other than an equality of proportion, as when there is an equal proportion between this and this, and that and that. And proportion is nothing other than the relation of one quantity to another. Quantity has the note of measure, something first found in numerical unity and thence deriving to every kind of quantity.

Unsurprisingly, we are now reminded of certain features of mathematical proportionality, and first that it is of two kinds, geometric and arithmetic. Let us set it forth schematically.

I. Kinds of Proportionality
    1. Geometric: a similar proportion (double, triple, etc)
        a. Disjunctive: $8 : 4 :: 20 : 10$ [four terms]
        b. Continuous: $8 : 4 :: 4 : 2$ [three terms]
    Disjunctive geometric proportionality enables us to find the mean in distributive justice.

    2. Arithmetic: exact numerical difference
        $9 : 7 :: 5 : 3$ (greater by 2)
    Arithmetic proportionality enables us to find the mean in commutative justice.

II. Properties of Proportionality
    1. Commutative
        Since $8 : 4 :: 6 : 3$ then $8 : 6 :: 4 : 3$
    2. Synecdoche
        $8 : 4 :: 6 : 3 = 8 + 6 : 4 + 3$

Thus the proportionality used in finding the mean of distributive justice will be geometrical and disjunctive. It cannot be continuous since two persons and two things are involved. The proportionality is a device whereby we can discover or come to knowledge of the mean.

    Distributive justice:
      2 hours of labor : 1 hour of labor :: \$20 : X = 2 : 20 :: 1 : 10.
    Commutative justice: to get the mean we add the quantities and divide by 2.
    Plato has 3 apples and Socrates has 1: $3 + 1 = 4 / 2 = 2$.

Beyond Quantity

Proportionals are useful in finding the mean of justice insofar as number means not just numbers but the numbered.

. . . numerus primo quidem invenitur in numero unitatum: et exinde derivatur ad omne aliud quantitatis genus quod secundum rationem numeri mensuratur. (*In V Ethics,* lect. 5, 939)

Number is found first in the number of units and thence derives to every other kind of quantity that is measured according to the ratio of number.

Wherever the quantified is, there proportionality can be.

Discrete quantity is divisible by one, continuous quantity by a minimum continuum. Since there is no least continuum, we use one inch or one foot or one meter, assigning 1 to the magnitude that will measure itself and others. One inch is not number, but numbered.

There is numbered number in magnitudes, motions, weights; colors are quantified thanks to their surface, which is continuous quantity.[1] What is the importance of this for proportionality?

Quia vero proportio est quaedam habitudo quantitatum adinvicem; ubicumque dicitur quantitas aliquo modo, ibi potest dici proportio. (*In de sensu et sensato,* lect. 7, n. 98.)

Because any relation of one quantity to another is a proportion, wherever there is said to be quantity of any sort, there proportion can be said to be.

Wherever there can be proportion, there can be proportionality. Proportion is found first in discrete quantity, then in continuous quantity insofar as it is numerable; then it is verified in those things that are called quantity *per posterius,* such as motion, time, weights; finally, in things like colors that are quantities only accidentally.

Proportionality is derived from the properties of numbers that always involve expressing a determinate distance, that is, a determinate relation of one quantity to another (*ratio propria*). A *ratio communis* (*quaelibet habitudo unius ad alterum*) is formed, which extends its use outside the realm of quantity.

1. *In V Metaphys.,* lect. 15, 984.

Although proportionality can be extended beyond quantity, that property of proportionality in the proper sense, commutability, does not travel beyond it.[2]

These considerations provide a tighter basis for the analogy of 'analogy' that we discussed in the previous chapter. *Proportio*, i.e., *analogia*, is verified first of all in discrete quantity, and then extended analogically through other senses of *quanta* and finally beyond quantity altogether. One of the meanings of 'analogy' is the very extended sense of the term expressing the proportion of one (or several) meaning(s) of a common name to another and controlling meaning of that term, that is, the analogous name. This doctrine of analogous names can be applied to 'analogy' or 'proportio' itself, as we have just seen; that is, 'analogy' has many related meanings, but only one of those meanings, and a very extended one at that, brings it about that 'analogy' means a plurality of meanings of a common term related *per prius et posterius,* and 'analogy' as meaning *that* can then be applied to the many meanings of 'analogy' itself, the *per prius* or *ratio propria* of which is the determinate relation of one quantity to another.

Proportionality was introduced into the discussion of justice as a device for discovering the mean. If proportionality can be extended beyond quantity, it can perhaps be a means of discovery elsewhere as well. Actually, it comes up crucially early on in the *Physics*.

Prime Matter Is Known by Analogy

Having reviewed what his predecessors had to say about the elements of change and the results of change (physical objects), Aristotle finds in the bewildering variety of accounts two latent points of agreement. Any change involves contraries and the subject of those contraries. This agreement is an indicator of where the truth may lie. Aristotle then takes up the matter himself.

At this point in his natural philosophy, Aristotle is interested in saying things that are true of anything that has come into being as the result of a change, any and every physical object. He must do

2. Cf. *In I Post. Analyt.* lect. 12, n. 8.

this, of course, by analyzing particular examples of change. At the same time, he will not be looking for what is peculiar to the example but for the way in which it tells us what must be true of anything whatsoever that comes into being by change. The example Aristotle employs is ingeniously chosen. "Man becomes musical," as Ross put it. We are asked to think of a human being acquiring an art, coming to know something. Little Charlie learns to play the cello. There was a time when he couldn't; now he can. A miracle has not occurred; he has painstakingly acquired the skill, and very well. This change, expressible as "A man becomes musical," can be stated in three different ways.

1. Man becomes musical.
2. The non-musical becomes musical.
3. The non-musical man becomes musical.

The difference is merely linguistic, and it consists in expressing the subject differently. The three sentences have grammatically different subjects, all of which refer to the same thing—the same subject in another sense of the term. There is another linguistic point that Aristotle wishes to make. The three expressions of the same change all exhibit the form "X becomes Y." But sometimes we say, "From X, Y comes to be." Can 1, 2, and 3 be translated into the latter form?

In one way, grammatically, they can, of course. When 3 is turned into

3a. From the non-musical man, the musical comes to be

and when 2 is altered to

2a. From the non-musical, the musical comes to be

we experience no sense of impropriety. We might as easily say the one as the other. But Aristotle asks us to reflect on our reaction by restating 1 as

1a. From man, musical comes to be.

The Greek equivalent of that restatement gave him pause, and the English does the same to us. Why? The suggestion of the form

"From X, Y comes to be" is that X ceases to be when Y comes to be. From this he concludes that the grammatical subjects of 2 and 3, unlike the grammatical subject of 1, do not denominate the subject of the change expressed, at least not *qua* subject.

Aristotle defines the subject of change as that to which the change is attributed and which survives the change. In 2, the change is attributed to non-musical man, but at the term of the change there is a musical man, non-musical man having ceased to be. In 3, the change is attributed to non-musical, and, again, when the change has occurred, non-musical is no more. Obviously, however, not only is the grammatical subject of 1 that to which the change is attributed but it also survives the change. It designates that of which it can be said: before he was not musical, but now he is musical.

From this analysis of the way in which we talk about the things we know, Aristotle now has independent grounds for saying that in this respect his predecessors were right; change seems minimally to involve contraries—non-musical and musical—and the subject of those contraries. Contraries are attributes that cannot simultaneously exist in the same subject.

It is at this point that Aristotle varies the example, and asks us to think of wood that from not being shaped has acquired a shape. Think of trimming logs and turning them into lumber. The choice of this example was fateful, since the Greek terms employed are *hyle* and *morphe*. From naming the constituents of one kind of change, they become equivalent to *hypokeimenon* or subject and *sumbebekos* or attribute. Change is then expressed as a subject or matter, from not having a form, coming to have that form. The not-having the form is not a simple negation—as in water is not capable of seeing—but a privation, the negation of something the subject is capable of having. (This is not a simple prediction, but a generalization from experience.)

The two examples prominent in Aristotle's analysis are a human being's acquiring an art and something natural being acted upon by a human agent and acquiring a shape it would not otherwise have had. Clearly Aristotle considers our own activities and interventions in nature as the best route for taking the first step toward understanding nature. In nature, there are changes in quality and quantity and place that clearly exhibit subject or matter, privation, and form. Of course, the point of the analysis is not simply to fuse different sorts of natural occurrence in a general statement. Aristotle's interest is to go from the generally expressed truth about things to more and more particular ones that express their differences. What they have in common is that a natural thing, an autonomous unity, a substance, from not having a quality or quantity or place, comes to have (or be in) it.

While Aristotle is glad to have clarified truths that were forced upon his predecessors, however obscurely, by the nature of the things they were talking about, he has to admit that in one sense he has been spinning his wheels. One of the complaints he has against his predecessors is that, although they were aware of the way in which substances can alter or grow or change place, they gave no account of how substances themselves come into being. And the major cause of this failure, he felt, was the baleful influence of Parmenides.

Is there substantial change, the coming into being and passing away of substances themselves, as well as changes of substance that involve the persistence and survival of the substance throughout the change? Aristotle is not interested in demonstrating that substantial change occurs, except in the sense that he will attempt to show us that we already think so. If there are autonomous things in the world, substances, the subjects of the kinds of change already spoken of, and if they sometimes are not, then are, then cease to be, then what is called substantial change takes place.

The problem of substantial change is the problem of its subject. To what could such a change be attributed? If it is some thing that survives the change, then it would seem that we are speaking of another instance of accidental change. Nor is it the case that from not being, substances just pop into being. The coming into being of a cow, an aspen, or a kitten, is lawlike. They do not just happen. We expect them to happen in certain conditions. A change cannot just take place without a subject, and, if there is a subject, there seems to be no substantial change. How can we explain what we already accept? By analogy.

The underlying nature is an object of scientific knowledge, by an analogy. For as the bronze is to the statue, the wood to the bed, or the matter and the formless before receiving form to anything that has form, so is the underlying nature to substance, i.e. the 'this' or existent. (*Physics* I, 7, 191a8–12)

If there are substances, and if they come to be, and if becoming involves a subject that from not having a form comes to have a form, then there must be some subject or matter involved in a substantial change.

Et dicit quod natura quae primo subicitur mutationi, idest materia prima, non potest sciri per seipsam, cum omne quod cognoscitur, cognoscatur per suam formam: materia autem prima consideratur subiecta omni formae. Sed scitur *per analogiam,* idest secundum proportionem. Sic enim cognoscimus quod lignum est aliquid praeter formam scamni et lecti, quia quandoque est sub una forma, quandoque sub alia. Cum igitur videamus hoc quod est aer quandoque fieri aquam, oportet dicere quod aliquid existens sub forma aeris, quandoque sit sub forma aquae; et sic illud est aliquid praeter formam aeris, sicut lignum est aliquid praeter formam scamni et praeter formam lecti. Quod igitur sic se habet ad substantias naturales, sicut se habet aes ad statuam et lignum ad lectum, et quodlibet materiale et informe ad formam, hoc dicimus esse materiam primam. (*In I Physic.,* lect. 13, n. 9)

He says that the nature that is first subject to change, that is, prime matter, cannot be known in itself since whatever is known is known through its form; prime matter, however, is the subject of every form. But it is known through analogy, that is, proportion. For thus we know that wood is something other than the form of stool and bed because it is sometimes under one form and sometimes under the other. Since, then, we see that that which is air sometimes comes to be water, we must say that something existing under the form of air is at another time under the form of water, and thus it is something other than the form of air, just as wood is something other than the form of stool and other than the form of bed. Therefore that which is to natural substances as bronze is to the statue and wood to the bed, and anything material and unformed to form—that is what we mean by prime matter.

It is not our present interest to pursue this subject further. Enough has been said to make our essential point. Knowledge by analogy, or proportionality, cannot be identified with analogous naming, even though it is a knowledge on which naming may be based. When we come to know X by analogy with Y, we tend to call X a Y. But to call X a Y is not necessarily to name it analogically.

We may come to know that 8 : 4 from a consideration of 4 : 2, but "double" is predicated univocally of both proportions. As a matter of fact, as often as not Thomas sees the *similtudo proportionalitatis* as productive of the metaphorical use of a term. There are many texts in which Thomas speaks of names applied metaphorically to God that are based on a *similitudo proportionalitatis*.[3] As fire destroys fuel, so God destroys impurity. Names said properly of God are said to be based on a *similitudo analogiae*.[4] As the sun is the principle of corporeal life, so God is the principle of spiritual.

Based on a similarity of effects. Things are said metaphorically of God "dicuntur de eo per similtudinem proportionabilitatis ad effectum aliquem" (*I Sent.* d. 45, a. 4; *ST,* Ia, q. 3, a. 1 ad 3).

A similarity of proportions can thus ground either a metaphor or an analogous name or, in the case of proportionality properly so called, a univocal name. Clearly in any similarity of proportions, one is taken to be prior and the other posterior . . .

Let this suffice to show that the analogous name, a kind of signification, is not to be identified with the discursive process called argument from analogy or knowledge from analogy. Sometimes the latter grounds the former, but not always. Thus there is only a *per accidens,* not a *per se,* connection between the two.

---

3. *Summa theologie,* Suppl. q. 69, a. 1 ad 2; *I Sent.,* d. 34, q. 3, a. 1 ad 2; ibid., d. 45, q. 1, a. 4; *II Sent.* d. 16. q. 1, a. 2; *III Sent.* d. 2, q. 1, a. 1, sol. 1 ad 3; *IV Sent.* d. 1, q. 1, a. 1, sol. 5 ad 3.

4. *II Sent.* d 16, q. 1, a. 2 ad 5.

NINE

ANALOGY AND PARTICIPATION

In this chapter, two matters are discussed: first, the so-called 'analogy of being'; second, the application of the doctrine of analogous names to talk about God.[1]

The Analogy of Being

The account that we have given of the analogous name, the one we profess to find in Thomas Aquinas, is objected to by many as dealing only with analogy in a logical sense, leaving its ontological and/or metaphysical side untouched. But, the objection continues, the real interest of analogy, and its true role in Aquinas, *pace* the proponent of the interpretation just alluded to, is metaphysical. It is not so much the analogy of 'being' that interests Thomas as the analogy of being.

What has been proposed has the merit of covering any and every

---

1. The two topics will be discussed only to the degree necessary to corroborate the overall point of this book.

name that can be said to be used analogously. If a name is said to be used analogously, this means that it has a number of *rationes* as predicated of the things that share it and these *rationes* are related *per prius et posterius*, so that one of them is called the *ratio propria*, and the others relate to it. Any other differences that arise from the specific content of these *rationes* are irrelevant. That is, while the meanings associated with 'healthy' in its analogous use have, of course, different contents from the meanings associated with 'form' or 'good' or 'being' in their analogous uses, these differences do not generate new types of analogous name.

Granted, it may be said, and let us pursue the point. Although 'being' as an instance of an analogous term is an analogous term in exactly the same (logically explained) way as 'healthy' and 'principle', when we turn to the content of the *rationes* of 'being' we are not interested in logical relations but in relations out-there, in the things that we know when we call them beings. It is the relation to one of the many existent things that constitutes what is meant by the analogy of being as opposed to the analogy of 'being'. Surely, it would be odd to wish to detain us at the level of logical relations between meanings when it is the relations among the things meant, as they exist, that interest the philosopher and, pre-eminently, the philosopher qua metaphysician.

Whose doctrine?

It is of course a lesser point but not without interest nonetheless to ask whose doctrine the analogy of being is. That is, is this being put forward as the teaching of Thomas Aquinas. Is it perhaps the teaching of Aristotle?

We saw in Chapter Two that discussions of Aristotle have been influenced by the Cajetanian interpretation, for example, those of Muskens and, to some degree, Ramirez. G. E. L. Owen, we saw, distinguishes stringently between analogous names (those with focal meaning) and analogy, which he says "is merely to arrange certain terms in a (supposedly) self-evident scheme of proportion. So, when Aristotle says in *Metaphysics* XII that the elements of all things are the same by analogy, the priority that he ascribes to substance is only natural priority (1071a35) and he does not recognize any general science of being *qua* being. There is no mention of pros hen legomena in XII, and none of analogy in IV."[2]

Owen is thus distinguishing a *natural priority* from *priority among a name's meanings,* i.e., focal meaning. Enrico Berti, on the other hand, discusses Aristotle within the ambience of the Cajetanian scheme and asks whether we find both analogy of attribution and analogy of proportionality in Aristotle. But he also asks if the analogy of being does not have Neoplatonic origins.[3]

This suggests the following hypothesis: Aristotle uses the Greek term ἀναλογία (and κατ' ἀναλογίαν) to refer to things arranged according to a natural priority, whereas Thomas uses the Latin *analogia* to speak of an order among the meanings of a common term.

Opposed to this hypothesis would be our earlier suggestion that, although Thomas uses *analogia* in a way that Aristotle does not (to speak of names said in many ways), he also uses the term to speak of the things Aristotle uses it to speak of. Thus, if Aristotle used the term *analogy* to speak of a real order of priority and posteriority among things, presumably Thomas would at least sometimes, e.g., when commenting on Aristotle, use the Latin term in that way too. We have seen that this is indeed the case, but a most interesting text is found in his commentary on Boethius.

In Boethii de trinitate, q. 5, a. 4

In commenting on Chapter 2 of Boethius's *De trinitate,* Thomas presents us, in Question Five, with a discussion of the kinds of theoretical science. In Article 1 he sets down the criteria according to which one can distinguish three theoretical sciences: natural, mathematical, and divine. Then, in Article 2, he discusses natural science, in Article 3 mathematics, and in Article 4 divine science. The question asked is this: Is divine science concerned with things separate from matter and motion?

The reader of Boethius may be puzzled by the introduction of this philosophical doctrine into a tractate dealing with the Trinity. Is the divine science that emerges from the threefold division the

---

2. G. E. L. Owen, *Logic, Science and Dialectic,* pp. 192–193 (=pp. 180–181).
3. See Chapter Two, above.

locus of the discussion of the Trinity? Thomas provides a solution to that puzzle in Article 4 by distinguishing between two kinds of divine science, two sorts of theology. His reasoning is as follows.

1. Every science considers a *genus subiectum* by way of its principles or causes. But principles are of two kinds:

a. Some principles are complete natures in themselves and are also the principles of other things. for example, celestial bodies are causes of earthly bodies, and simple bodies are causes of the complex. Such complete natures can enter into one science as the principles of its subject and into another as the subject of the science.

b. Other principles are not natures complete in themselves but are only principles of natures. For example, one is the principle of number, point of line, form, and matter of physical body. These principles are treated only in the science of the things of which they are principles.

2. There are common principles of any determinate or definite genus that embrace all the principles of that genus. For example, all beings insofar as they communicate in being (that is, have being in common) have principles that are common to all beings. But such principles are common in two ways:

a. *uno modo per praedicationem,* e.g. 'form' is predicably common to all forms;

b. *alio modo per causalitatem,* e.g. numerically one sun is the cause of all generable things.

The article continues as follows:

Omnium autem entium sunt principia communia non solum secundum primum modum, quod appellat Philosophus in XI (= XII) Metaphysicorum, omnia entia habere eadem principia *secundum analogiam,* sed etiam secundum modum secundum, ut sint quaedam res eaedem numero existentes omnium rerum principia, prout scilicet principia accidentium reducuntur in principia substantiae, et principia substantiarum corruptibilium reducuntur in substantias incorruptibiles, et sic quodam gradu et ordine in quaedam principia omnia entia reducuntur. (*In Boethii de trin.,* q. 5, a. 4, c)

There are certain common principles of all beings not only in the first way, which the Philosopher speaks of in the *Metaphysics,* saying that all beings have the same principles according to analogy, but also in the second way, such that there are some things numerically the same which are the principles of all things, insofar namely as the principles of accidents are reduced to the principles of substance and the principles of corruptible substances reduced to incorruptible, and thus in a hierarchical order all things are reduced to the same principles.

This line of reasoning is now applied to divine science. There are entities that, since they exist separate from matter and motion, are more actual and complete than other beings. Divine science will deal with such beings. It turns out, however, that there are two divine sciences. There is a science called divine, the theology of the philosophers, which studies such separate being as the cause and principle of being as being; and there is another divine science, that based on Scripture, which studies such separate being as its subject.

This extremely interesting discussion casts light on our question. There are two kinds of principle that may be said to be common to all beings. Some things are predictably common to all beings, and they have the unity of universals. But there are also causes that are common to all beings, preeminently the divine cause. God's causality extends to all created beings, and they form an orderly hierarchy with secondary causes producing effects that in turn are secondary causes of further effects, although God is the first and immediate cause of every being. For our purposes, what is of particular interest in this discussion is that Thomas speaks of analogy when it is a question of predicable community, but he *does* not call the real hierarchy of being an analogy of being. (We notice that, when he does speak of analogy, he invokes Aristotle's *Metaphysics*, Book Lambda.) On the basis of this text in the *De trinitate*, I will venture to suggest that Thomas does not use the term *analogy* to speak of the real hierarchy of being, but it is the ordered progression of creatures from God that is meant by the "analogy of being."

Objection   Why not simply admit that we can proceed from the analogy of 'being' to the analogy of being? If we concede that we mean the same thing by calling 'being' an analogous name as we mean when we call 'healthy', and so forth analogous names—that is, that it has a plurality of meanings related in an orderly way to one meaning that is invoked to explain the other meanings—*none-*

theless, when we examine the content of the meanings of 'being', our attention is directed to being, that is, to the real order, not to the logical order. And there it is not simply the case that substance is first called 'being', but it is primarily being. It is not simply that the meaning of 'being' as said of accident refers us to its meaning as said of substance, but accident really depends on substance in order to be. Thus, if we do not get hung up in the logical order, an inspection of the content of the meanings of 'being' must direct us to the real order.

Respondeo   This objection has the merit of not asking us to recognize a new type of analogous name but rather to see that there is a real dependence of accident on substance and that this dependence can ground a use of the term 'analogy', namely a real relation of dependence. As we now know, when 'analogy' means such a real relation, it does so thanks to a meaning that is prior to the meaning of 'analogy' that points to the order among the meanings of a common term.

So far so good. In a plausible fashion the "analogy of 'being'" leads on to the "analogy of being," with 'analogy' in the first phrase referring to logical relations (= analogous name) and 'analogy' in the second referring to real relations. St. Thomas may never have used the term 'analogy' of the latter but he *could* have, given his account of the way *proportio* is extended from mathematical relations to any kind of relation.

What we have here is a happy coincidence between the *ratio propria* and what is first *secundum esse*. Alas, that coincidence indicates both the limits and the danger of this proposed passage from the logical to the ontological. It cannot provide us with a basis for the great cascade of being set before us in *De trinitate*, q. 5, a. 4. This is best seen by turning to a brief account of how analogous naming is applied to talk about God.

The Divine Names[4]

We name things as we know them. We know God through His effects. We name Him from his effects. That is why the question of divine names is always a question of how names are common to, shared by, God and creatures. Whenever he poses this question, Thomas reminds us of the way names can be analogously common to many and then applies this to names common to God and creature.

He gives us reason to distinguish between negative terms, relative terms, and what we might call positive terms.[5] It is only the last that raise the question of analogous community. Negative terms, e.g. immaterial, certainly name God from creatures but simply by denying of Him a trait of some creatures. Relative terms, e.g. Lord, or cause, relate him to creatures but do not tell us about Him as He is in himself. That is, the meanings of 'Lord' and 'cause' are intrinsically dependent upon something other than God, but God as He is is not dependent on anything else. Therefore such names do not express what God is. There is left what we are calling affirmative names, e.g. being, good, wise, intelligent, powerful, and so forth.

Analogous Divine Names

How is it possible to name God otherwise than from creatures? To say that some divine names are analogous is just as such to say that they are shared by God and creatures, and, given the rule that we name as we know, the application of these names to God is dependent on their previous application to creatures. In order to understand what is meant by saying that God is wise, we must consider what we mean by calling Socrates wise. In order to understand

4. Cf. *The Logic of Analogy*, chapter 9, pp. 153–165, and "Can God be Named by Us?" in Ralph McInerny, *Being and Predication: Thomistic Interpretations* (Washington, D.C.: The Catholic University of America Press, 1986), pp. 259–286.

5. Cf. *ST*, Ia, q. 13, a. 2. Thomas is here confronting the views (a) that all the divine attributes, even positive ones, tell us what God is not rather than what he is, or (b) that he is the cause of the created perfection named by such an attribute as 'good'. Thomas maintains that the positive attributes tell us, however imperfectly, what God is. But there *are* negative attributes, such as immaterial and timeless, and there are relative attributes, like Lord and cause.

what is meant by calling God just, we must consider what we mean by justice in human interactions, and so on with all the analogous divine names.

The Structure of the Ratio[6]

The account meant by a name cannot be simply another name. To say that clothing means raiment is to say that these terms are synonymous, but what is the one meaning they share? That meaning must be complex, and definition is often what is meant by ratio or meaning. The definition is composed of genus and difference—locating it among similar things and distinguishing it from them. *Every ratio is complex.*

It is the formal element in the ratio that the term chiefly signifies: rational rather than animal, since rational sets men aside from other animals. This is the denominating form, the *res significata,* that from which the name is imposed to signify. *Every ratio signifies a res in a given way.* This was exemplified earlier by the difference between concrete and abstract names: white is that which has whiteness, whiteness is that thanks to which white things are white. But it is only concrete terms that are predicated of individuals, so we settle on *id quod habet humanitatem* or *id quod habet albedinem* as the model of the conjunction of *modus/res* in the ratio. Then we can contrast univocal, purely equivocal, and analogous terms by saying that (a) the term said univocally of many has the same *res* and *modus*; (b) the term said equivocally of many has different *res significatae*; (c) a term used analogously has the same *res significata* and different ways of signifying it, *modi significandi.*

Divine Names

Just as, when many things are named healthy analogously, we have a plurality of meanings so that the same *res* (health) is involved in them all but there are different modes of signifying it (subject of _____; cause of _____; sign of _____) with some modes invoking the primary mode or *ratio propria,* so too is it with names common to God and creature. The question of analogous names arises be-

---

6. I recall here some highpoints from Chapter 3 above.

cause creature and God share a name. Socrates is wise; God is wise. Whenever he approaches this situation, Thomas recalls the doctrine of analogous naming and invokes the example 'healthy'. The clear implication is that 'healthy' exemplifies a kind of meaning also to be found in names shared by God and creature. In its two occurrences, 'wise' has the same *res signficata* (wisdom) but different modes of signifying it. In Socrates' case, to call him wise is to say that he has acquired a virtue thanks to which he sees things in their proper order and that he could lose this virtue. On the other hand, we do not attribute wisdom to God as a quality he acquires or even one that he simply possesses eternally.

The common name, as used to signify what a creature is, will have a meaning that is complex and, if a definition, will consist of genus and difference. The account of an adjective, a word signifying an accident concretely, must include the subject of the accident *ex additione*.[7]

A Dionysian Process

From the pseudo-Dionyisus, Thomas learned the threefold way to understanding analogous talk about God.

Via affirmationis: God is wise.
Via negationis: God is not wise.
Via eminentiae: God is eminently wise, super wise; the mode of his wisdom is beyond our comprehension.

This process makes it clear that, from the point of view of understanding the application of the term to God, we must invoke its creaturely use. But God's wisdom is not dependent on there being any creatures; rather the wisdom of creatures is dependent upon God. So we want to say that there is an order *per prius et posterius secundum impositionem nominis* that does not express the order *secundum esse*.

In short, in names analogously common to God and creature, the creature is the *per prius* and the *ratio propria*, since we must make reference to the creaturely meaning to fashion its meaning as applicable to God. At the same time, we are aware that what we last

7. Cf. *In VII Metaphys.*, lect. 4, nn. 1342–1343.

name is what is ontologically first. Any coincidence of the *per prius secundum impositionem nominis* and the *per prius secundum esse* is just that, a coincidence, *per accidens*.

The Asymmetry of Predication and Causality

Insofar as one has in mind what Fabro calls horizontal analogy, there is a coincidence of *ratio propria* and the ontologically first in the case of 'being'; but, when it is a question of what Fabro calls transcendental analogy, there is a dramatic asymmetry between the order of naming and the order of being. Those who talk of the analogy of being fight against this asymmetry and sometimes even suggest that the meaning of a term as said of creatures is dependent upon its meaning as said of God. What is true, and what should be clearly stated, is that in positive names common to God and creature, although the name according to its *ratio propria* is said first of creatures and only secondarily of God, the *res significata* of such names exists first and preeminently in God—God is wisdom *essentialiter*—and is participated in by the creature, who *has* wisdom. The *ordo rerum* in this case is exactly the opposite of the *ordo nominis*. This reversal of order is neither productive of a new kind of analogous name nor the only properly analogous name. Indeed, if we started with examples of names shared by creature and God to explicate the logical doctrine, our procedure would be (etymologically) preposterous. Exactly the same account of analogous naming applies to 'healthy' and to the positive divine attributes. That the doctrine more obviously and manifestly fits 'healthy' is just what we would expect. Neither our knowledge nor our language (nor our accounts of language) are proportioned to the divine, and they must be stretched to cover this limit case. But it is this stretching and this limit case, knowledge of the source of all being of whom finally we know what he is not rather than what he is, that is the ultimate point of philosophizing.

The Point of the Book

Cajetan got Thomas wrong because he misread the text from the *Sentences* and because he tried to make Greek usage regulative of the Latin use of the loan word *analogia*. My first thesis is that Aristotle never used the Greek term *analogia* and its cognates to express what Thomas means by analogous names. Thus far, that is merely a terminological claim, not a claim that what Thomas calls analogous names and what Aristotle speaks of as things said in many ways amount to different doctrines. On the contrary, we have argued that they are the same.

My second thesis is that Thomas never speaks of the causal dependence in a hierarchical descent of all things from God as analogy. That is, terminologically speaking, there is no analogy of being in St. Thomas. There is, of course, the analogy of 'being'. This is not to say that Thomas did not hold what others call the 'analogy of being', but he could not have confused that with analogous naming. If he had employed this usage, he would have recognized that this was possible only by employing different meanings of the analogous term 'analogy'. He would not have confused the two meanings, pressing the real proportion or analogy of creature to God into analogous naming, as if it were a type of it. He would point out that the coincidence of the *ordo nominum* and *ordo nominis* is adventitious; this coincidence happens to occur only with some examples of things named analogously. If the analogous name sometimes has this coincidence and sometimes not, the conclusion is that such considerations are *per accidens* to the analogous name.

At this point, the major arguments of my interpretation may be seen to be cogent, yet the reader may feel a lingering dissatisfaction. The result may seem to be simply more terminological information. What difference does it make? Just this: that, if the 'analogy of being' refers to real relations, so that what is first is the cause of what is secondary, and if 'analogous names' involve an ordered plurality of meanings of a common name in which the first, controlling meaning, the *ratio propria*, is not the cause of the rest, the difference is as important as the difference between the logical and real orders.

Thomas Aquinas took this difference between the order of our knowledge and the order of being to be decisive as between Plato and Aristotle. He accuses Plato of confusing these two orders and assuming that what is first in our knowing is first in being. Any confusion of the logical and real orders comes under the same criticism. A correct understanding of Thomas on analogy saves him from the grievous mistake he attributed to Plato. The point of this book is far more than terminological precision.

SELECT BIBLIOGRAPHY

For the works of Thomas Aquinas, I have used the Leonine edition when it was available and the manual editions of Marietti when it was not. For Aristotle I have used *The Complete Works of Aristotle*, edited by Jonathan Barnes, two volumes (Princeton: Princeton University Press, 1984).

Ashworth, E. J. "Signification and Mode of Signification in Thirteenth Century Logic: A Preface to Aquinas on Analogy." *Medieval Philosophy and Theology* 1 (1991), 60–61.

Aubenque, Pierre. "Néoplatonisme et l'analogie de l'être." In *Néoplatonisme: Mélanges offerts à J. Trouillard*, 63–76. Fontenay aux Roses, 1981.

———. "Les origines de la doctrine de l'analogie de l'être." *Les études philosophiques* 103 (1978), 3–12.

Boethius, Anicius Manlius. *In Categorias Aristoteli*. PL 64.

Brentano, Franz. *Von der manigfachen Bedeutung des seienden nach Aristotele*. Freiburg, 1862.

Cajetan, Thomas De Vio Cardinal. *Scripta Philosophica. De Nominum Analogia. De Conceptu Entis*. Edited by P. N. Zammit, O.P., and P. H. Herin, O.P. Rome: Angelicum, 1952.

Casetta, Giuseppe, ed. *Origini e Sviluppi dell'Analogia da Parmenide a S. Tommaso*. Firenze: Edizioni Vallombrosa, 1987.

De Muralt, A. "Comment dire l'être? Le problème de l'être et de ses significations chez Aristotle." *Studia Philosophica* 23 (1963), 109–62.

DeRjik, L. *The Place of the Categories in Aristotle*. Assen: Van Gorcum, 1958.

Dubarle, D. "La doctrine aristotélicienne de l'analogie et sa normalisation rationelle." *Revue des sciences philosophiques et théologiques* 53 (1969), 3–40, 212–32.

During, O., and G. E. L. Owen, eds. *Aristotle and Plato in the Mid-Fourth Century. Papers of the Symposium Aristotelicum*. Goteborg: Elanders Boktryckerie Aktibolag, 1960.

Fiedler, Wilfried. *Analogiemodelle bei Aristoteles: Untersuchungen zu den Vergleichen zwishen den einselnen Wissenshaften und Kunsten.* Amsterdam: Gruner, 1978.

Grenet, P. "Saint Thomas d'Aquin a-t-il trouvé dans Aristote '*l'analogia entis*'?" In *L'attualità della problematica aristotelica.* Atti del Convegno franco-italiano su Aristotele. Padua: Antenore, 1970, 153–75.

Hirschberger, J. "Paronymie und Analogie bei Aristoteles." *Philosophische Jahrbuch* 68 (1960), 191–203.

John of St. Thomas. *Cursus Philosophicus.* Edited by B. Reiser, O.S.B. Vol. 1. Turin: Marietti, 1933.

McInerny, Ralph. *The Logic of Analogy.* The Hague: Martinus Nijhoff, 1961.

———. *Studies in Analogy.* The Hague: Martinus Nijhoff, 1968. *Metafore dell'invisibile: Ricerche sull'analogia.* Contributi al XXXIII Convegno del Centro di Studi filosfici di Gallarate. Brescia: Morcelliana, 1983.

Montagnes, Bernard, O.P. *La doctrine d l'analogie de l'être de après saint Thomas d'Aquin.* Paris–Louvain: Nauwelaerts, 1963.

Moreau, Joseph. "La Tradizione Aristoelica e *l'Analogia Entis,*" in *Metafore dell'invisibile* (see entry above), 91–96.

Muskens, G. L. *De vocis analogiae significatione ac usu apud Aristotelem.* Groningen: J. B. Walthers, 1943.

Owen, G. E. L. *Logic, Science and Dialectic.* Collected Papers in Greek Philosophy by G. E. L. Owen. Edited by Martha Nussbaum. Ithaca: Cornell University Press, 1986.

Owens, Joseph. *The Doctrine of Being in the Aristotelian Metaphysics.* 3d edition. Toronto: Pontifical Institute of Mediaeval Studies, 1978.

Philippe, M.-D. "Analogon and Analogia in the Philosophy of Aristotle," *The Thomist* 33 (1969), 1–74.

Pinchard, Bruno. *Métaphysique et semantique: Autour de Cajetan.* Etude et Traduction du 'De Nominum Analogia'. Paris: Vrin, 1987.

Ramirez, Jacobus Maria., O.P. *De Analogia.* Edited by Victorino Rodriguez, O.P. Madrid: Instituto de Filosofia "Luis Vives," 1970–72. Trendelenburg, F. A. *Geschichte der Kategorienlehre.* Berlin, 1846.

INDEX